Table of Contents

Introduction   7

Chapter 1
Learning from the Past to Inform the Present: 13
Maya Hieroglyphic Writing
Overall Reading Order of a Complete Maya Text   18
Verb First in the Maya Sentence Structure   19
Verb First within Computer Syntax   20
Individual Hieroglyphs and Computer Icons   22
Reusing Hieroglyph and Computer Icon Elements   24
Organising Maya Hieroglyphs into Three Distinct   26
Categories
Representational Hieroglyphs   28
Phonetic Hieroglyphs   31
Maya Hieroglyphs which use a Mixture of   34
Representational and Phonetic Elements
Conclusion   36

Chapter 2
Simple Words and Visual Metaphors   39
Partial Writing Systems   45
Isotype   47
Standardising Symbols (ISO)   52
Base Lexical Icon Elements   55
Conclusion   58

Chapter 3

Designing Icons for the Graphical   59
User Interface

Visual Reading Order within a Compound Icon   61
Conflict, Contrast or Harmony within a Compound Icon   64
Using Space within a Compound Icon   69
Using Type within a Compound Icon   74
Reusing an Icon Element within a Compound   80
Conclusion   83

Chapter 4

Computer Compound Icons and their Families 85

Consistent Use of Symbols   88
Case Studies   90
Case Study 1: Marine Security Limited   91
   The First Element: Background Circle   93
   The Second Element: M   93
   The Third Element: Underlining the M   94
   The Fourth Element: S   95
Case Study 2: Print and Publish Belize   96
Changing a Letterform into a Symbol Element   97
Computer Compound Icons and their Families   100
Conclusion   111

Chapter 5

Evaluating Representative and Abstract   113
Computer Compound Icons

The ABC's of Graphic Symbols   115
The ARC Interface   125
ARC Evaluation   128
Returned Data from the Report Logs   132
Conclusion   134

Chapter 6
Navigating Interfaces 135
User Goals and Sub-goals 135
Interfaces that use Real World Metaphors 152
Icons from around the World 164
  Africa 166
  Asia 168
  Australasia 171
  Europe 173
  Europe - United Kingdom 175
  North America excluding USA 175
  United States of America 178
  South America 180
Conclusion 181

Bibliography 183

Index 189

Acknowledgements

This book would not have been possible had it have been supported by the help, advice and encouragement of many people. I am indebted to Dr. Howard Leathlean who read every chapter diligently offering constructive criticism and academic leadership which has allowed me to reappraise this text; also to Dr. Adrian Vranch without whose technical knowledge and innovative approach especially during Chapter 5 which has made unique methods of data collection possible. Sadly Dr. Linda Schele of the University of Texas died in 1998 at the age of 53, without her inspiration and enthusiasm for all things Maya this book would not have formed the way it has. Clive Chizlett and Professor Masoud Yazdani have also been influential in shaping this book – without Clive's letters many ideas would have been untried. I now promise to write back. Masoud has encouraged me to actively participate at conferences which again has helped me to focus on what my intentions actually are. Thanks also to Phil Cutler who systematically went from ISP to ISP around the world, building a data bank of compound icons for Chapter 6. I still have visions of him telling me that he's nearly up to Israel. Finally, last but definitely not least, thanks to my wife Glynis who patiently endured all of this. I promise that this is the last PhD that I ever do or write up as a book. To the rest is life.

Trademarks

This book is dedicated to:

Glynis, Lois and William Honeywill

Introduction to a Visual Language for the World Wide Web

It needs to be stated first that visual language for the GUI (Graphical User Interface) needs clarification as to how its parts are described. Graphic designers talk of basic elements, and that elements can come together to form other elements that then have a relationship with other elements until the design is complete. Linguists such as Michael Stubbs (1980, p.12) consider that the grapheme is the smallest unit of meaning, but that readers decode from letters to phonemes, but after individual letters have been learned readers 'might decode at a level of syllables, morphemes or words'. Elements which make-up an icon compound are no different, one element might contain lines or curves which are then joined with other elements to form a complete compound, in the same way users of interfaces might decode the icon at a level of elements or the completed compound icon. How meaning is assigned by both decoder and encoder is no different from semiotics as determined by Umberto Eco in his 1976 book *A Theory of Semiotics*, but a re-definition of terms that are relevant to computer interfaces. To explain this further of how one set of rules may be adapted or expanded, for example, Clive Chizlett identifies Eco's six sets of relationships, which are relations between concept and ideograph, symptomatic, metonymic, metaphoric, vectrol, phonetic and transformational to envision a seventh set which is systemic in his unpublished paper the *Silent Messenger* which explores the Chinese concept-script and its implication for the development of context-governed inter-lingual message-exchange.

The *Chambers 20th Century Dictionary* describes semiotics as the 'theory of sign systems in language' and that there are three kinds of sign – those which look like what they represent, abstract forms which represent the essence of an object and indexical where the referent sign implies its meaning through an indirect relationship with what it represents. Aaron Marcus (1992, p.52) describes a 'trail of muddy footsteps in a front hallway' as an index sign that children have entered the house, because it is a regular occurrence and they are always being told to take off their shoes, so they are the logical cause. Finally a symbol is a sign that can be arbitrary in its appearance and does not necessarily need to have its connotation understood. What it denotes is through learning. Compound icons used on computer interfaces can be a mixture of all three, and make computers function through visual semantics (what these icon and icon elements appear to represent); syntax (which refers to grammar as a visual reading order within the compound icon), and lexical forms (elements within the compound icon that appear to be in regular use). Then finally there is the pragmatics of our ability to view these compound icons through a computer interfaces.

The purpose of this book is to speculate on the developmental route of a visual computer languages and how computer users comprehend interfaces. What has become apparent is the natural development of visual language for interfaces which now form the World Wide Web. No organisation or individual has decided what it should be, it has merely evolved. Compound icons found on websites in North America or Europe are no different from those that appear on interfaces in Central America or Asia. This is not a haphazard arrangement – many factors have enabled this to happen since modernism at the beginning of the 20th century, or indeed 6,000 years earlier with pre-cuniform Sumerian. These influences outside of interfaces, and the transactional nature of using computers has created a visual language through context, contact and a shared code. The context describes the reason for the interaction which is normally transactional between humans and computer interfaces; contact is how the interaction is performed (point/click) and code is the agreed method of communication during interaction (text, compound icon and its lexicon). This book does not measure or factor probabilities of language development – it analyses different visual writings systems to compare their use and possible implication for interfaces. This is undertaken in two main ways. First, by undertaking a small-scale investigation of Maya hieroglyphics to learn from the past and see how this informs computer interfaces; and secondly the first half of this century is looked at and its implication for computer interfaces of the second half of this century studied.

The approach to computer syntax is to introduce Maya hieroglyphic writing in Chapter 1 as a small-scale investigation to be compared with other visual writing systems and natural written language. This does not attempt to imply that Maya writing has had any influence upon interfaces, indeed when the Apple Lisa was introduced in 1983 Maya hieroglyphs were still mainly undeciphered with scholars debating their content in terms of language or simply calenders. The reason to choose Maya hieroglyphs is because it is now known that it never lost its visual origins to write ideographically, phonetically or more usually as a mixture of both. In order to compare systems, hieroglyphs and English grammar are explored for their use of syntax and how this can be applied to computer compound icons. The comparison identifies some similarities and differences between verb, object and subject use, but more importantly their use of consonants. Also certain other commonalities can be identified from the Maya observation of the natural world, and how they interpreted this through the use of their metaphors. Frogs, especially when squashed, have no denotive or connotative association with birth in cultures other than the Maya. In their context and shared code this has the power to convey the appropriate concept, and is no different from another culture's equivalent. It is an opportunity to appreciate why this visual writing system could be used in a precise way.

Chapter 2 questions the assumption that nouns (objects) and verbs (actions) as visual metaphors are readily understood. First, a questionnaire is undertaken using computer compound icons out of their intended context. These icons are elements from a specific program, icon elements randomly selected from many programs, and a symbol system used outside of computer interfaces. All except the first and final category would have text associated with them. It is argued that icons should be able to communicate independently of written language and that understanding of icons need only be approximate and not exact. It must also be remembered that the purpose of 'icon driven' interfaces is so that general and functional information can be instantly accessed, therefore the relationship between symbols and natural written language are explored. However, there are systems that are expected to function independently of natural written language. Indeed, for some, language would impede function slowing down the operator when speed of operation is essential, such as operating a difibulator when patient information needs to be rapidly processed through compound icons.

It has long been acknowledged that new mediums allow for a change in design possibilities, both good and bad, and computer interfaces are no different. It is also important not to forget past or present communication mediums that have built up principles of how best to present and organise how legibility and readability are achieved. What can be learned from this and applied to a new medium is dealt with by returning to fundamentals established by other modes of communication. Therefore Chapter 3 recognises this, and also the fluid nature of interfaces being capable of describing the original in different ways and possibly not what its designer had initially intended. Problems can become an opportunity to be solved in ways that are unique to interfaces. To establish possibilities computer compound icons are measured against other applications of design, for example how magazines are viewed overall to enable the reader to be directed around pages. Using established principles can help evaluate what carries over, what can be adapted to form new principles, and just as importantly what does not apply at present.

The layout of a magazine has a less obvious connection to the design of compound icons. What is obvious would be symbols that are designed for corporate identities. Both might appear the same by possibly using a combination of elements, or one object to imply a meaning, or have a meaning assigned through regular exposure. Also corporate identity symbols are normally abstract, while computer icons attempt to represent what their denotation actually is. Therefore, the connotation of a corporate identity symbol might possibly be difficult to understand, even unimportant, but important to computer icons that rely upon representational recognition. Computer icon elements that become associated with meaning are normally through regular exposure as part of other icons, because of this they appear to develop as an overall part of visual syntax. To help understand these differences symbol design for a corporate identity programme is explained through case studies of how an identity is created. Chapter 4 is concerned with family completeness when icons are grouped together on interfaces. In this respect families of computer compound icons have a closer semantic relationship with the development of sign systems that establish meaning for elements which are then used throughout a scheme. However, symbol design informs sign design which in turn helps in the construction of computer compound icons and their families.

If something works well, it can go unnoticed and remain the same, and this is probably true of human-computer interaction, ever since Kays notion of how SmallTalk might possibly work. Microsoft helped to establish the Apple approach of how users communicate their intention to the central processor, and it has fundamentally been that way ever since. Chapter 5 will show that a baseline for the natural selection for visual syntax has formed which continues to form part of the overall interaction. If this is so, then having learned the approach of how to use something once, it then becomes more of the same for using interfaces with other metaphors – simply put, skills transfer. Therefore, how users learn is central to Chapter 5. Observing people using computers might suggest that those who don't ask for assistance or an explanation are probably achieving their task. This is an assumption – an empirical approach would be to get behind the interface and track, monitor and generate a computer report on how users react to different interface metaphors which range from abstract to representative and among their own family compound icon groups, to discover without bias what precisely happens.

Chapter 6 identifies that in order to learn a system of navigation through an iconic interface there must be incentives. People who own microwaves probably understand functions that allow them to heat-up, cook, defrost and so on. There are other functions which are probably known to people who don't own cookers and wish to create gourmet meals. If there is no gain from using something then other alternatives that are already known might be tried, or even not attempted. This chapter undertakes to make some sense of this by analysing how users perform when asked to use software that is familiar to them by identifying functionality that they would normally not use. This is then extended to how magazines try not to alienate their readership and retain navigation through a publication and what the implication might be for interfaces. Finally, everything written throughout each chapter is not definitive, each merely suggests a direction of enquiry.

Learning from the Past to Inform the Present: Maya Hieroglyphic Writing

Thomas Erickson pointed out that interface design normally follows the traditional approach of art and design, which requires reworking to refine an idea through visual playfulness until a solution has been achieved. Erickson (1990, p.12) wrote that 'design by symmetry works by juxtaposing concepts that are similar at a very deep level – the concepts are symmetric in terms of some deep structure or underlying process. Once the underlying symmetry is established, designers attempt to extend the symmetry farther, using what is known about one domain to suggest new ideas about the other'. Therefore, the aim of this chapter is to explore the Maya visual writing system and how hieroglyphs work as representation or as a precise phonetic meaning, which are unlike computer compound icons which remain utilitarian. Hieroglyphs and English grammar are compared for their use of syntax and how this is applied to computer compound icons. The comparison will expose some of the similarities and differences between all three to identify verb, object and subject use which is used here in the sense of language as metaphor for human-computer interaction. The advantages and disadvantages of a writing system that has remained visual, yet has progressed from ideographic to phonetic will be explored to establish if there is an implication for computer interfaces.

Jill Hamilton (1997, p.7) stated that 'it doesn't look as though the pace of technology is slowing down – the technology is already in place to allow for the production of systems which relay and receive video telephone messages via your computer – providing facilities for such applications as video tele-conferencing, remote job interviews by selection panel, international training seminars or multiple opinions from medical experts around the world as a remote surgical procedure is actually taking place'. Communication through computers and the convergence of mass media through WebTV now knows few barriers. The television viewer has a passive relationship with a television programme. Computer users do not view a computer, instead there is a 'doing' relationship. In order to do things with a computer there must be a dialogue between computers and users. Iconic metaphors used as the language of the Graphical User Interface have only been in recent existence. Can the development of computer iconography as visual language aid communication across transnational language and cultural barriers, and if so where should this begin?

Before the development of an intuitive computer interface all human interaction with computers was through command-line instructions. This required a high level of computer understanding – computers were for computing and not for ordinary working tasks. With the advent of the Apple Lisa, learning complex Boolean logic was no longer required to operate a computer.[1] People with real needs, such as those identified by Hamilton can now execute complex code sequences without the need to recall correct command-lines, and like operating the computer itself, the design process of any program requires that each stage is expressed simply before complex line-commands are written. Under the title *The Icon Revolution*, Gunther Kress (1995, preface) writes that:

[1] Steve Jobs and Steve Wozniak released the Apple Lisa II in January 1983. It had an interface that was based upon metaphors of the real-world.

> While Gutenburg's revolution made language in its written form central, the current revolution is taking us both backwards and forwards into hieroglyphics. Whether this is in the introduction of emoticons through the exploitation of the visual potential of typographic elements, or the proliferations of the use of icons in so-called written texts, or indeed in the treatment of (verbal) text itself as merely an item in a visual composition, in new-modal, multi-media form of text, what is happening is a fundamental challenge to the hitherto unchallenged cultural centrality of written language.

[2] In correspondence with Clive Chizlett, who is a member of International Society of Typographic Designers's working party on typographic teaching. Chizlett writes that, 'Japanese notation: four character-sets. Firstly, some 2000 Kanzhi ideographs taken from the Chinese writing system. Secondly, a 71-character syllabary (the hiragana character-set). Thirdly, the 71-character syllabary (the katakana character-set). Fourthly, the romazi or roman alphabet with numerals and punctuation signs. Katakana is used to express important words (a-me-ri-ka). Hiragana is used in two ways: to help children how to say the ideographs, but also used to give grammatical inflection throughout clauses'.

Indeed, the need for mediated human-computer-human interaction challenges the centrality of written language. Geoffrey Sampson (1985, p.26-45) questions the possibility of constructing a writing system out of symbols that have no necessary connection with language. Michael Coe (1992, p.17) cites William Wang (1981, p.223-236) and answers this by pointing out that certain Chinese characters were adopted by the Japanese for their sound value, although both spoken languages are different. The Japanese took the structure of Chinese and used selected graphical elements to form the basis of their writing system. Japanese signs are used in two ways – first, to write the words in full, and second, to assign smaller characters around the main character to aid meaning.[2] Modern Chinese concept-scripts might have lost their similarity with the objects that they originally depicted in their archaic form – the archaic for 'the spoken word' and the 'horse' appear abstract, but their connotation is identifiable once explained (Chizlett, 1999) (figure 1).

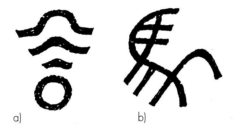

a)   b)

Figure 1. a) In its archaic form the shape of the mouth and sounds coming from the mouth are apparent once explained, b) the horse rising up on its back legs (reproduced from Chizlett).

Richard Gregory (1970, p.137), a Professor of Bionics at the University of Edinburgh, is interested in the psychology of seeing. Gregory writes that 'early Chinese ideograms are remarkably similar to Egyptian hieroglyphics though separately invented . . . the ideographic scripts became, gradually, systems of writing related to the spoken words in use at the time. This occurred first with the Mesopotamian, Egyptian, Cretan and

Hittite scripts, which all developed sound associations' (see Chapter 5). At present computer icons do not have a phonetic structure they are utilitarian which is similar to early ideographic writing systems. However, the structure – of how a writing system works can have parallels with the development of computer icons.

Hieroglyphic writing first appeared in the Nile Valley about 3100BC and did not change in its essential logographic form until its decline. This Egyptian method survived 3400 years of use, longer than any alphabet system. It was free from ambiguity, with only a small percentage of the 2,500 individual signs in common use. Hilary Wilson (1993, p.30-33) tells us that if the Egyptians needed new words there was a sufficient vocabulary of signs that could be joined with phonetic complements to express meaning – the system had rules. Other hieroglyphic systems such as the Maya developed independently of any 'old world' influence, yet, like the Egyptian system contained a mix of logographic and visual phonetic elements. This system also utilised a smaller percentage of glyphic elements rather than the full array, which would have been available to the scribe. In a glyph for glyph showdown the Maya writing contained less elements than the Egyptian system, so the Maya encoders and decoders had less to learn. To construct a visual writing system that is not linked to any particular language, with unambiguous usage, could as Kress suggests, enable mediated human-computer-human interaction across national boundaries, but should this be more than encapsulated concepts? We should indeed look back to look forward. Tatiana Proskouriakoff's (1960, p.454-475) achievement in identifying that Maya hieroglyphs conveyed meaning was not through attempting linguistic decipherment, but through the identification of structure.[3] In the same way as Wang has identified, it is not the meaning of Maya hieroglyphs that is important to the development of a language for the Graphical User Interface, but the structure of the Maya writing system. Empirical data collected from the many Maya inscriptions that have been deciphered now makes the structural analysis of the writing system possible.[4]

[3] The Maya structure was first published by Yuri Knorosov in the 1950s. Unfortunately, the publisher had added Communist propaganda on how communism had succeeded over the capitalism. This made it difficult for scholars to associate themselves with Knorosov's theory in an America that was anti-communist. Knorosov, Y. 1952 Drevniaia pis' mennost' Tsentral'noi Ameriki. *Sovietskaya Etnosgrafiya* 3 (2) p.100-118. Published in English in 1958 by *American Antiquity* 23 (1), p.284-291.

[4] The technique of structural analysis can be accredited to Dr Linda Schele, as cited by T. Jones, C. Jones, 1996, *Maya Hieroglyphic Workbook*, Humbolt State University, pvii, unpublished.

Figure 2. Lintel 8, Yaxchilán. 'He captured him Jewelled Skull Bird Jaguar and he sacrificed him.' (reproduced from Jones and Jones).

In 1974 one of the pivotal Dumbarton Oaks mini-conferences about the Palenque inscriptions identified sentence construction as temporal statement verb/subject. By applying this grammatical structure to a Maya text the decipherment of glyphs was made easier when their value as verbs, subjects or objects was known. Linda Schele and Mary Miller (1986, p.324) stated that 'with this structural pattern as a starting point, it was possible to identify glyphs as verbs, subjects or objects, even when the signs occupying those structural positions were undeciphered. It was found for example, that the Maya combined two sentences in one, as in the English sentence "Bird Jaguar captured and sacrificed Jewelled Skull." In the inscriptions, the same statement would be arranged, "He captured him Jewelled Skull Bird Jaguar and he sacrificed him." To an English speaker, it is obvious in the English sentence that Bird Jaguar was the agent who performed two actions, but without reference to the normal order of object and subject'.[5] The visual nature of the Maya system allows for the detection of meaning; who the actor was, what was the object and what was the action taken by the actor (figure 2, above).

[5] This refers back to Tatiana Proskouriakoff's analysis of historical data at Yaxchilan, T. Proskouriaoff, 1963, Historical data in the inscriptions of Yaxchilán, *Esudios de Cultura Maya*, 3, p.149-167, Mexico City, published in English.

Overall Reading Order of a Complete Maya Text

Before any structural comparison between Maya hieroglyphs
and computer icons can begin it is important to outline how
the language system works. The reading order of any Maya text
block is normally top left, and then down two glyphs at a time.
However, the reading order can sometimes be structured differently (figure 3). This can only be confirmed by knowing the
position of the date glyphs which always preceed each sentence.
After the dates have been located and the reading order established the system uses an ordered grammar structure. The text
structure might be different from text to text, but the hieroglyph
had to work in a precise way because many visual elements had
phonetic values, and therefore a set of rules for reading. In this
respect Maya hieroglyphs have progressed from ideographic to
phonetic as either separate hieroglyphs or a mixture of both.
Computer compound icons have developed towards greater
utility, are self-contained and strive to be self-explaining. They
have not been designed to work as rows of icons that then
make-up a sentence.

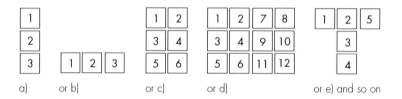

Figure 3. Common reading order. However, the rules are not fixed, text reading can
be reversed or arbitrary. The reading order of a text can also be mixed. For
example, the Palenque Palace text uses a), d) and e).

Maya inscriptions will normally begin with the Initial Series
Introductory Glyph (patron), followed by the Long Count (the
date) and Calender Round (confirmation of the date by using a
different method of time correlation). The Long Count places
the text into a linear cumulative time frame. This linear time
frame is measured from the base zero. Each sentence within the

inscription will then normally begin with a Distance Marker (Distance Number Introductory Glyph) followed by a Distance Number. The Distance Number refers back to the time difference between the sentence and the Long Count. This is then followed by a Calender Round confirming the date which will be one of 13 numbers and one of 20 names. Both numbers will change daily until base 13 and base 20 have been reached. All glyphs after the Calender Round and before the next Distance Marker will be the sentence (figure. 4). Each new sentence begins with a verb followed by the object and then the subject (figure. 5).

Marker   Distance Number   Calender Round   Verb   Object/Subject

Figure 4. The Maya sentence structure. (reproduced from the Palenque Palace inscriptions).

a) Verb   b) Object   c) Subject
She was born   she, Cherished   Lady Kin Ahau
                                  of the Turtle,

Figure 5. After the date and marker glyphs have been removed (reproduced from Bricker, deciphered by Schele).

Verb First in the Maya Sentence Structure

By placing the Verb (the doing word) after the date, the sentence now reads; 'Todays date is – the event is – the object and subject of that event are'. The hieroglyphs can therefore say, 'she was born' (figure 5a), 'she, the Cherished One of the Turtle' (figure 5b), 'Lady Kin Ahau' (figure 5c).[6] Verbs appear to be

[6] Stele 3, Piedras Negras, D6, C7 and D7, full-translation by Dr Linda Schele as cited by M. Coe, 1992, *Breaking the Maya Code*, Thames and Hudson. Part-translation with glyphs reproduced from V. Bricker, 1986, *A Grammar of Mayan Hieroglyphs*, Middle America Research Institute, Tulane University, p.218.

19

mainly representative of their meaning with phonetic complements to the main sign to confirm that meaning. For example, the glyph verb known as 'Squash Frog' represents birth. Our equivalent to the squashed frog is how we visualise an unborn baby. Culturally, the concept would have been familiar to the Maya. If the main sign was used in a contemporary context, how an unborn baby would appear in the womb could be used to represent the direction or location of maternity information. The position of an unborn baby is familiar to us through its media usage to describe not only the human condition of pregnancy, but also of vulnerability, innocence and so on (figure 5a page 19, and 6 drawn by a different scribe).

The structure of a written English sentence is subject-verb-object. All declarative sentences have a subject and a verb, but not necessarily an object. According to Tom and Carolyn Jones (1995, p.66) the structure of the Maya text is verb-subject or verb-object-subject. This is similar to the necessary syntax required to interact with computer interfaces. The use of computer visual syntax allows the user to recognise objects on the desktop so that associations can be made with all the possible choice of actions. Simply put, one method would be for users to select an icon that visually suggests what it will do, and then apply the appropriate action through the pull-down menu. However, there are other relationships between users and the interface that are not underpinned by written language and depend on visual metaphors, such as an application programs tool box. These normally have a verb-object or a verb-object-subject syntax followed by the action of the object.

Figure 6. The birth glyph 'Squash Frog' can best be viewed by turning the page 90° anti-clockwise. Note that the eye of the frog is in the middle (reproduced from the Palenque Palace inscriptions).

Verb First within Computer Syntax

The verb which is used here in the sense of language as a metaphor for system use is probably the most used and important part of computer syntax, and because computers are used for tasks the mood of the verb is in the imperative, and its subject is always in the second person because you are the user. For example, in Adobe Photoshop the compound icon used to represent the verb 'crop' is based upon the photographic L

[7] Chizlett writes that the four commands might be compressible into the command 'crop', but is the indirect object grammatically. Therefore the imperative verb, denote, isolate, store display (the) object, framed area, denoted area, isolated area, stored area (with) the instrumental indirect object, frame tool (by) the unvoiced joint passive subject, interface (and) unvoiced joint active subject, the user.

frame, with a broken line set at 45° angle to suggest anamorphic scaling. The L frame is a photographer's tool to crop the picture being exposed to photographic paper. Cardboard Ls are also a graphic design studio tool that allows the designer to see how a picture would appear after being cropped and resized. When a picture has been digitised for use as a computer file it could be from many sources such as an unedited transparency or a PhotoCD and so on. The crop tool (verb) is positioned over the picture (object) which is then click/dragged to the appropriate position by users (subject). After the crop action, the picture will have a different size. (figure 7).[7]

Verb
Crop

Object   Subject   Action
Picture   Crop   Cropped

Figure 7. The verb 'crop' is based upon the photographic L frame.

From this it is apparent that desktop metaphors can form other relationships and change the order of the syntax depending upon their use. The pointer or I-beam within a program or on the desktop can select an object and then select the appropriate verb from either a menu or a palette. A folder on the desktop is not a verb, users iare not expected to do anything other than placing and removing objects to it and from it, and when necessary naming the folder. By identifying that verbs describe the action and that the subject does the action, and that the object has the action done to it, the metaphors used to describe the computer desktop forms three distinct parts of visual language,

21

but in different combinations for both individual icons or as a sequence. Therefore, icons need to describe themselves as:

1) An object for choosing an action.
2) A verb that does something to an object with the subject of the verb.
3) An icon with no verb (such as a folder), but which represents an object or the subject of a verb.

Individual Hieroglyphs and Computer Icons

The smallest single element of meaning within a glyph can be representative of an object in the real world, or a phonetic unconnected to its visual representation. These elements come together to form the next highest unit, the Maya compound hieroglyph.[8] These units of meaning are wedged tightly together within the hieroglyph. David Kelly (1976, p.209) cites Hermann Beyer and suggests that one of the most important conclusions of Beyer's study 'was that the order of elements is far more important than the particular way in which they are arranged in glyph blocks. Thus, some affixes may occur to the left of a main sign or above it, both being interpretable as pre-fixed elements'. Position within a Maya hieroglyph is important because of the representative and phonetic mix to spell out a precise meaning. Therefore, the reading order of a hieroglyph is normally left prefix, unless there is a superfix which occurs normally as a prefix with a reading order that begins from the top then to the left, followed by the centre (main sign), and finally right postfix. If the glyph has two postfix elements the right postfix is normally read before the bottom postfix. This is merely a general, and not a definitive guide to illustrate the reading order (figure 8).

The smallest single element of meaning within a computer compound icon is normally representative of an object in the real world, or part phonetic such as a single word or letter that has taken on meaning beyond its phonetic value. These elements come together to form computer compound icons. Like the Maya system computer icons feature a main sign and

[8] P. Barnard, T. Marcel, 1978, Representation and understanding in the use of symbols and pictograms, R. Easterby, H. Zwaga (eds) *Information Design*, John Wiley and Sons, p.57. Describe the use of elements within compounds as having the 'status of morphemes in natural language'. T. Jones, C. Jones, *Maya Hieroglyphic Workbook*, p.98. Describe glyph elements within the compound hieroglyph as morphemes.

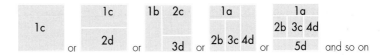

Numbers indicate the normal reading order. Letters indicate:

a) **Superfix** *(normally read first if present)*

b) **Prefix**   c) **Main Sign** *(could have infix)*   d) **Postfix**

d) **Postfix**   *(normally read next if present)*

Figure 8. a) and b) Prefixes can be affixed to the left of the main sign or above, c) The main sign takes up most of the space within the glyph, Infixes can be placed within the main sign and d) Postfixes can be suffixed to the right of the main sign or below.

can have other visual elements prefixed, infixed or postfixed. Normally within a computer compound icon there is no established reading order other than visual priority. The position of elements within the computer compound icon are dependent upon size relationships to convey an idea. If the order of the syntax is incorrect, the meaning becomes difficult to understand. For example, if users were to remove a file from a folder, in English the phrase would be, 'the file was removed from the folder'. The sequence of selection of icons need only be the folder, and the file. If the metaphor for folder (object) was not first in the reading order (figure 9c), then the intended meaning that it is a folder that contains this kind of file would become confused. Therefore, programs such as Adobe Photoshop will have a folder to imply the content (figure 9d), which will contain the application program (figure 9e) and other folders inside of the main folder that are associated with the functionality of the program (figure 9f).

Figure 9. below (a) Can be any folder containing files, (b) Maya glyph as folder to contain Maya related files, but it is not apparent that it is a folder (c) Combining a and b into a visual reading order, this folder contains Maya files. The following compound icons d, e and f demonstrate the practical application of visual priority in a reading order.

a) Folder   b) Folder   c) Folder   d) Folder   e) Application   f) Folder

Reusing Hieroglyph and Computer Icon Elements

By establishing the reading order of a glyph it becomes apparent that units of meaning which make-up the glyph block are used in other ways to form new glyphs. As illustrated below, elements of the glyphs can be used to pictographically represent what it is in one glyph, yet as a sound value in another with no association to its original representation. Therefore by glyphs elements can be representative of real world objects or abstract, or a mixture of representative elements and phonetic complements associated to the main sign within the compound hieroglyph (figure 10). Repeat elements, such as the affixed hand, can be recognised as making some form of gesture independently of specific language for both systems (figure 11). Of this Phillip Harling and Alistair Edwards (1997, p.75) write that 'the gestures we make are able to both clarify what is spoken, and also able to describe objects (their size, location in space, relative motion etc) more intuitively and with less effort than spoken language. This suggests that we should consider our innate capability for gestural communication and study how gestures are used in human communication, and then apply what we have learnt to the human-computer interface'. Clearly the Maya considered the importance of gestures to signify meaning and this is also true of computer interfaces. The Maya hand affix like its computer icon element counterpart is mainly representative, (when phonetic *k'o*, hand down, *chi*, hand horizontal) and 'doing' something.

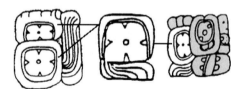

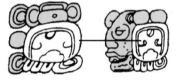

Kin (1 day) Logogram (Sun) Doubled, Main sign and Prefix   Winal (20 days) Main Sign and Postfix

Figure 10. Using elements of meaning to form new glyphs (reproduced from the Palenque Palace Text except the first Glyph which has been reproduced from Jones).

Figure 11. Appropriate elements such as the hand survive through their ability to be unambiguous, adaptable, and a help to clarify meaning especially as a verb (glyphs reproduced from Bricker).

For reasons of utility written communication normally progresses from being representational towards an abstract representation of sound. The Maya did not reduce concrete representational meaning to abstract representation for sound. Maya writing retained visual representation of objects familiar to them for both phonetic and representative glyph elements. Yet, like a phonetic system the Maya reused a fixed amount of elements in different combinations to convey meaning beyond written words. Similar to a word in English the Maya scribe could interchange semantic elements within a hieroglyph. This had the advantage of precise meaning through phonetic affixes underpinning a broader message that placed the entire text into context (see Chapter 5). Norman Hammond (1982, p.298) cites Michael Coe, who suggests that, 'phonetic complements were often attached to ideograms to help in their reading, either prefixed as a representation of the initial sound of the sign, or postfixed as the final consonant' (figures 12d and 12e). This made the overall reading of a text unambiguous to the Maya because there was always a reference to phonetics that was precise and could not be interpreted in any other way.

Fundamental elements of computer compound icons continue to be reused, retaining their representational value, and becoming more sophisticated as the pixel intopolation of the software and screen quality develops allowing for refined images (see Chapter 3). This allows fundamental units of meaning to progress towards greater utility, such as the hand holding simple tools to imply what kind of program application the icon represents (figures 12a and 12b). The XObject icon represents catching a Macromedia Lingo Script error and is not intended to be a user application, but an application that the program uses (figure 12c).[9] Similarity with Maya writing and their use of real-world images differ to that of computer icons. It can retain representation such as scattering blood from the hand (see Chapter 2), or become a phonetic element within the hieroglyph, 'It ended' (figure 12d), or with additional elements, 'It ended, the 5th tun' the completion of a 360 day cycle (figure 12e).[10]

a) Make a note b) Download a digital picture c) XObject to catch an error d) It ended e) It ended, the 5th tun

Figure 12. Computer and Maya hand preforming a task, however Maya hands can have other semantic values. (glyphs reproduced from Bricker)

[9] An example would be the Audio CD XObject v.2.3 which catches a CD Audio Access error which hangs the playSegment for 10 seconds and returns an ioErr as the error. XObjects also reduce the scripting.

[10] The final two hieroglyphs are reproduced from a complete text at Piedras Negras, Stela 3 positions F4 and F9.

Organising Maya Hieroglyphs into Three Distinct Categories

The main structure of Maya writing can be organised into three distinct categories. Maya inscriptions have two main parts to the structure, this was then used in three different ways to convey an overall concept, a precise phonetic description, or a mixture of both. There are also other variations which parallel visual communication systems. Computer compound icons assign more than one representation for the same meaning (figure 13), There is no precise way of implying that these are application programs, their denotation is helped through context. Therefore, a user wishing to compress a file might understand the implied meaning of a filing cabinet being reduced, (figure 13a) and a user wishing to create multimedia would understand what is implied by the directors chair and the megaphone (figure 13b).

a)   b)

Figure 13. Different Application programs.

[11] East is new life (sun rises), west is the underworld, home of the gods and death.

[12] Cited by Coe L. de Rosny, 1876, Essai sur le déchiffrement de l'écriture hiératique de l' Amérique Centrale, Paris

Reading order
1 phonetic
2 representational

Figure 14. The hand that covers the disc, completion of the sun, *ch'kin* 'west' (reproduced from Coe).

Maya hieroglyphs can have more than one representation for the same sound. Maya hieroglyph polyvalence also assigns more than one meaning to an object. Of this Jones and Jones (1995, p.96) writes that 'the day sign for Manik', when it appears without the day sign cartouche in a non-calendrical context, is *chi'*. In the Maya mind set direction has meaning, the west is where the sunsets and the home of the underworld.[11] Michael Coe (1992, p.149) credits Léon de Rosny[12] for the identification of the directional glyph for 'sunset' or 'west' as the hand that covers the disc, and that the combination should be read as 'completion of the sun', *chikin*. Coe goes further and deciphers part of the hieroglyph (the hand) phonetically as the sound *chi* (see phonetic table, page 32), placed above the logogram *kin* (1 day), and therefore reads 'west' (figure 14). Yet the directional glyph east still retains the disc in the same position as west. Therefore, the phonetic/logograph mix must be as Coe suggests. It would be convenient for the hand to be pushing the sun below the horizon as Léon de Rosny suggests. Only images that have phonetic values can achieve this. Pacal, who ruled Palenque for the main part of the sixth century A.D., retained his shield within representative, representative/phonetic and phonetic glyphs. In the example below all three main methods of writing proclaim that he was lord protector of Palenque (figure 15). Each single unit of meaning such as the shield can be used in different ways other than in the spelling of Pacal (see figures 15 page 28, and 18 page 32). Both systems are pragmatic in their use, always being used within context – computer interfaces – stele in Maya plazas.

Therefore, the semantic value of hieroglyphs can be organised into three methods of writing:

a) sufficient glyphic representational elements to convey an overall concept (figure 15a), or

b) a precise phonetic description (figure 15b), or

c) a mixture of both (figure 15c).

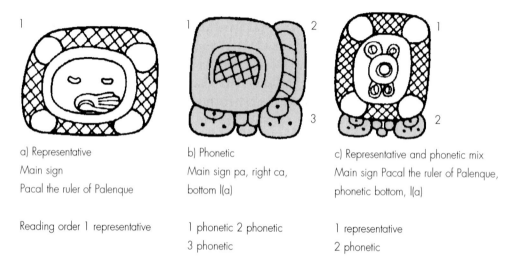

a) Representative
Main sign
Pacal the ruler of Palenque

Reading order 1 representative

b) Phonetic
Main sign pa, right ca,
bottom l(a)

1 phonetic 2 phonetic
3 phonetic

c) Representative and phonetic mix
Main sign Pacal the ruler of Palenque,
phonetic bottom, l(a)

1 representative
2 phonetic

Figure 15. Three different operative levels for the spelling of the same word 'Pacal(a)' (reproduced from Coe).

Representational Hieroglyphs

Some Maya hieroglyphs have self-evident meanings in a Maya context. These core Maya semantic ideographs have no linguistic referent although as discussed with the day sign Pacal's shield they can have a sound value added. However, hieroglyphs that are used to represent what they denote are in this respect no different from computer compound icons. Maya ideographs were more economical to write semantically as common terms to communicate a generalised, culturally familiar concept rather than phonetically spelling out the message. An example would be the Palenque Palace inscription recognition that there is a fundamental change to a child at the age of seven. This is

[13] For deciphering Maya Glyphs and using Calenders go to www.halfmoon.org

celebrated with an event known as the Deer Hof (9.10.18.17.19 2 Kawak 12 Yax).[13] At the time of writing this Maya scholars were still unclear about the nature of the event, but what is important is the observation that there is a change in an individual's perception of self, this real-world event is then recorded, using the deer, and the hand scattering droplets of blood to denote sacrifice, also the seven circlets postfixed to record the age of Hok Chitam II at the time of this ceremony (Jones, 1997). By noting what the Maya have said and observing children who are around seven years old it can be appreciated that certain social skills and taboos take on an importance to them, any younger and Kan Hok Chitam II would not have appreciated the implication of his right of passage (figure 16a) and eventual assession to the throne as Cham Balhum II.

a) Age of seven ceremony   b) Ascension

[14] The title Ball Player has been added by Kan Hok Chitam II to Pacals titles after his death. A ruler would not be expected to play this game of life or death. The Palenque Palace inscription that he has commissioned is probably there (positioned behind his throne) to explain his use of the title, and also to show his lineage from Pacal, past ruler and Ball Player.

Figure 16. a) The Deer Hof event glyph. Prefix, the deer. Main sign, blood event. Postfix, seven. b) Prefix, the sun. Main sign, blood event. Both use the blood event elements to be read as a ceremony (reproduced from the Palenque Palace inscriptions).

The text from the Palenque Palace inscription goes further and tells of the ascension of Makina (Great Sun) Cham Balhum II, who is actually Kan Hok Chitam II. The purpose of taking another name as successor to the throne and then metaphorically killing off the name allows Kan Hok Chitam II to take that name in his honour and therefore retain honorific titles that have been awarded in death (9.13.10.6.8.5 Lamat 6 Xul). Before this point is reached in the text Kan Hok Chitam II honours the memory of Pacal by additional titles added to his name such as Ball Player (9.12.11.5.18 6 Et'nab 11 Yax).[14]

The ascension hieroglyph uses elements that are used in the Deer Hof event. The hand juxtaposes its position with the sun (day sign above hand, left prefix) and blood scattering dots are postfixed to the main sign indicating that the ascension was also accompanied by a blood sacrifice (figure 16b, above). This demonstrates the precision in which this writing system could be used as Cham Balhum II uses this as a political text to confirm his right to the throne, but also lineage to Pacal who was one of the great rulers of Palenque, and who lived for over 80 years.

Observation of events in the real-world has produced many glyphs that have a representational value. However, representation can be misunderstood. Computer compound icons can explain their meaning further by becoming motion dynamic. For example, an English reader might book a flight through Macau International Airport in China, because they offer the combination of flights and times that are required. If the booking desk is called up from the Internet, and the interface is all in Chinese, users are only able to proceed if there are metaphors that can be recognised that will allow users to change the required information into English, or in the case of Macau, Portuguese. If users cannot read Chinese, English or Portuguese they can possibly understand what is being implied and navigate to the correct web pages within the site, yet further interaction other than navigation merely becomes guess work (1999). A static icon can suggest what its function is, however the meaning might not be verified until the icon becomes motion dynamic, and so confirms the meaning, by 'acting out' the 'doing' action. Maya hieroglyphs could not be animated, however, confirming the meaning by doubling the message was practised by them. The glyph 'two moons' or two months ago has the hand pulling the two old moons to one side. There is also a prefix which contains two dots which confirm the message (figure 17).[15]

Figure 17. Two months ago (reproduced from Bricker).

[15] Stele 3, Piedras Negras, position A6.

Phonetic Hieroglyphs

Within the Maya system polyvalence was a regular occurrence with many units of meaning having more the one value either semantically or phonetically, as a compound hieroglyph or as a grapheme (element) within the glyph, or as a ideographic element which has a sound value and does not represent the object as it is depicted in the real world. The Roman alphabet has developed as a phonetic abstract representation of sound. Gone are the many signs that represent different meanings. It is impossible to associate the Egyptian (c.4000BC) pictographic drawing of the bull, or the pre-cuniform Sumerian (c.3500BC) simplified lines which represent the bull, as the Roman letter 'A' or of a sound value (see chapter 5). Both can be traced to the Phoenician (c.1200BC) 'alpha' – it is at this point that hieroglyphic scripts converge and split. The Roman script develops the vowel, and the Arabic develops the semivowel. The Maya scripts had no such opportunities of convergence to influence their development.

John Sören Petterson (1996, p.40) explains that an abstract form of writing such as a phonetic alphabet is the last sequence in the evolution of a writing system, 'while semasiographic and ideographic devices are the first things to be utilised by mankind'. Patterson is right in his general observation of the development of writing systems, but with no Phoenician equivalent as a catalyst, the Maya script retained its visual origin for phonetic elements probably because the spoken language of the Maya (except for dialect and so on) was primarily the same, the Phoenician point of departure was through adaption to different spoken languages. John DeFrancis (1989, p.51) points out that 'the poorer a writing system is in phonetic representation, the more it compensates . . . by greater use of nonphonetic devices' (see Chapter 2). This is not so in the development of the Maya system.

The Maya phonetic table can allow the scribe to use more than one glyph element to spell out meaning. Part of the phonetic table illustrated demonstrates that the sound 'ba'

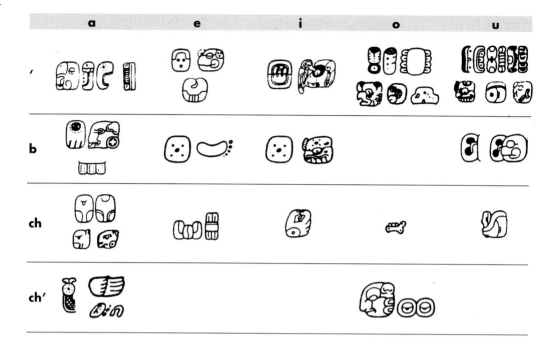

Figure 18a. A part example of the phonetic table (reproduced from Jones). Note that ' indicates a glotteral stop.

Figure 18b. Part of Maya phonetic table for the sound values of 'pa' (2), 'pi' (3), 'po' (1) and 'pu' (1) (reproduced from Jones and Jones).

has three glyph elements, whereas the sound 'be' has two (figure 18a). Pacal would have been a well-known figure as one of the great rulers of Palenque, this is because the glyph was widely used, his 'flower shield' could lend the language the sound value for 'pa'. The phonetic table gives two values for 'pa', both 'pa' glyph elements retain the stylised marking that represent the jaguar while other glyphs such as 'pi' can have very different representations for the same sound (figure 18b).

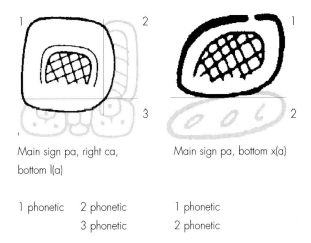

Main sign pa, right ca,
bottom l(a)

Main sign pa, bottom x(a)

1 phonetic   2 phonetic
              3 phonetic

1 phonetic
2 phonetic

Figure 19. Phonetic spelling for Pacal (ruler of Palenque) on Stele and Pax (month) as cave painting (19a reproduced from Coe, 19b reproduced from Bricker).

Not only could sound values be added to hieroglyphic elements, further confirmation of the meaning could also be added because of the visual nature of particular phonograms. For example, 'at (penis-title) (figure 20a) which is a sacrificial title associated with the Maya practice of blood letting by piercing the penis with a sting ray spine so that blood loss would cause an hallucination giving rise to a serpent vision event where the giver, normally the ruler, would have a vision due to blood loss. What is important here is that the ruler Yax Pasah of Copan, of which this penis title glyph is in association (as an honorific) takes on three additional meaning for the same hieroglyphic element, *yox'at* (scarred penis), *tox'at* (scarred penis) (figure 20b) and *yotox'at* (very scarred penis) (figure 20c). The hiero-glyph denotes the the title holder has either had a vision or has had many visions over a period of time depending on the scar's inscribed on the glyph element (this element can be found at other sites). Ronald Baecker and Ian Small (1990, p.256) suggest that computer compound icons can have coding of degrees 'of "dullness" to indicate age; newest documents are brightest and most visually salient, while older documents become progressively duller' (figure 19d). This notion does not

33

need to confine itself to long periods of time, and therefore does not need to be a metaphor for an aging process, it can be for shorter periods of time where the transactional nature of interfaces would best describe priorities (time required to download a file, print, fax or email a document) (figures 20e and 20f), quantities (text length within a document) and so on.

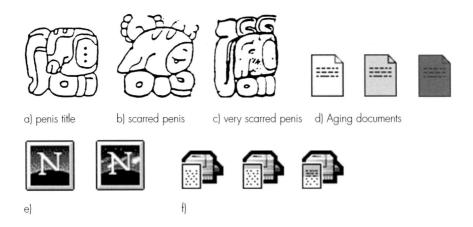

a) penis title   b) scarred penis   c) very scarred penis   d) Aging documents

e)   f)

Figure 20. a) to c) Further denotation could be added to hieroglyphic elements because of their visual nature, d) Baecker and Small also suggest that there are semantic implications for computer compound icons such as the age of a document, e) indicates that files are still being downloaded, and f) implies the progress of a document being printed (hieroglyphs reproduced from Jones and Jones).

Maya Hieroglyphs which use a Mixture of Representational and Phonetic Elements

Morphological units of meaning can mix both representational and phonetic elements. Stephen Houston (1989, p.25) explains that visual representation mixed with 'phonetisim simply made writing more precise, without replacing the rich imagery of pictorial signs'. Of this Jones and Jones (1995, p.95) write that 'one aid in decipherment stems from the the Maya habit of affixing CV (consonent vowel) phonograms to CVC logograms as phonetic compliments. There is for example, a glyph that seems to be associated with the sky . . . it turns up in texts that accompany pictures in which the upper margin of the scenes (where one might expect the sky to be portrayed) . . . this "sky" glyph is almost always suffixed by the phonetic complement -*na'*. The Maya word for sky is ka'an, the implication of this is that it emphasises the final consonant, other texts prefix *ka*- within the sky compound hieroglyph, therefore according to Richard Hudson (1984, p.9) 'it makes relationships explicit which would otherwise be implicit'. Put simply by him 'that only consonantal letter (or sound) that can precede a *t* at the beginning of a word is *s*. (Compare the ordinary words sting and stay with the impossible combinations *lting* and *rtay*). If the consonant does not match the reading of the representative element within the compound hieroglyph, then the decipherment is wrong. The hieroglyph balam 'jaguar' can therefore be written in several ways depending on how the phonetic element was to be used by the scribe (figure 21). The Maya according to Jones and Jones (1995, p.95) had the habit of 'substituting different forms for the same sound', and it is this that gives Maya hieroglyphs a visual richness'.

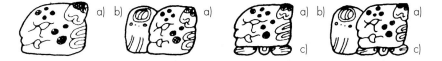

Figure 21. Four ways to say balam 'jaguar', three confirm that it is the jaguar. a) balam, b) ba (see phonetic table page 34), c) m(a) (reproduced from Coe).

There is no apparent equivalent of interface compound icons using phoneticism in such a way. The Maya spoke one language therefore CVC relationships could work. There is however, a further possible explanation as to why the Maya had variation of hieroglyphic elements. The Maya system appears to have the confidence to use visual homophones to 'play' with the reader, and imply the emotion of the speaker. Typography today does precisely this – there are over ten thousand fonts which can be formed into more than two thousand type families that visually shout, whisper, demand and so on. These families can be classified into eight basic groups – Old Style, Transitional, Modern, Square Serif, Sans Serif, Decorative, Script and Gothic. With so many combinations and possibilities at the disposal of designers, choice can become subjective if there is not a fundamental understanding of typographic design which informs an objective choice. It is not the quantity of typefaces that designers use that creates an aesthetically pleasing page, it is an ability to recognise why typography has subtle differences. By knowing this designers can use typography effectively and in the right context. Adrian Frutiger (1989, p.3) who brought together alphabet, logotype and symbol design through human concern explains slight typographic differences by stating that, 'You may ask why so many different typefaces. They all serve the same purpose but they express mans' diversity. I once saw a list of Médocs all of the same year. All of them were wines but each was different from the others. It's the nuances that are important.' Maya writing was limited to the scribe classes, and like typographic designers, would know how to interplay these hieroglyphic elements, if not for aesthetic then for semantic reason or a mixture of both.

Conclusion

The Maya hieroglyphs sentence structure is verb, object and subject, but it must also be recognised that other language systems use other combinations. Individual hieroglyphs, such as the verbs describe doing events. These events normally contain sufficient information to describe an entire sentence. The value of mixing phonetic elements within the compound hieroglyph helps to confirm what the glyph denotes, used in combination with other compound hieroglyphs there is no ambiguity in meaning. Computer compound icons are not intended to work as rows of information giving a collective message. Computer icons are visual units of information which are self-contained but not necessarily self-explaining because different images can represent the same thing. Position within a Maya hieroglyph is important because the representative and phonetic mix construct a precise meaning. Computer compound icons are representative, the position of elements within the icon are dependent upon a reading order through size to convey an idea which will always be in context. These elements should conform to the rules of visual and not grammatical syntax if the icon is to be understood, size is important within computer compound icons and position is dependent upon the combination of elements to aid meaning (associative positioning). Maya hieroglyphs do not necessarily need to be in context to be understood, understanding is through learning the rules for grammar and the meaning of the elements used. Computer icons are always used in context as a visual prompt for what it might possibly imply.

In English it is not necessary for all sentences to have an object. For example, 'she is walking', 'she is walking the dog' and this can be true of computer compound icons. However, unlike English, computer icons also change the order of the relationship depending upon their use. Establishing a method for visual reading can only aid the message if the compound icon is as Stuart Mealing and Masoud Yazdani (1990, p.133-136) explain 'graphically clear, semantically unambiguous, without linguistic bias (culture, race?), adaptable (open to modification to express shades of meaning), simple (perhaps created within a 32 x 32 pixel matrix)'.

The Maya system works because it is the only written language system available to both encoder and decoder, therefore both invest time in learning that system, and no other. Computer compound iconography works when designers invest time learning to understand how to manipulate elements as visual language, aided by context. To extend the meaning of icons will require more learning investment for users possibly through the establishment of elements that have only one meaning as base graphic elements, but probably not a standardised system for position within the compound icon. In this respect language can progress from ideographic to phonetic, or towards greater utility. One lesson from the Maya is the consonant relationship, for a compound computer icon users could make the distinction between a basket and a casket, because as an icon it would possibly look the same, in this example the consonant could be prefixed but not postfixed because both words end in *t* which would show no difference. This is not dissimilar as to how a child acquires reading skills by seeing the first letter of a word in association to that object. However, this would not aid universal understanding because a written language would need to be decided. At present anything other than utility would defeat the purpose of computer compound icons, users do not need precise language to operate computers or navigate interfaces.

Simple Words and Visual Metaphors

Many computer programs assume that visual nouns and verbs are understood. Computer compound icons and icon elements from a specific program, icon elements randomly selected from other programs, and a symbol system used outside of computer interfaces are evaluated for their meaningfulness. This is achieved through a questionnaire that has icons which would normally have natural language underpinning, and icons that stand alone. For the purpose of the questionnaire no language association has been assigned to any compound icon. This chapter will then explain the relationship between compound computer icons and natural written language. The understanding of what an icon represents can be open to a 'fluid' translation, therefore why certain symbols need to be underpinned with language are investigated. Other symbol systems appear successful without any association to natural written language. These language independent symbol systems are expected to be understood regardless of the appearing dennotive and connotative values of that symbol. Visual language systems such as ISO/IEC (International Organisation of Standardisation/ International Electrotechnical Commission) are regulated and are expected to be learned by users. ISO/IEC symbols are compared to systems where written language has been used, this will facilitate an analysis through comparison of word and image relationships that form human-computer interaction.

Stuart Card, Thomas Moran and Allen Newell (1983, p.4) write that 'the human-computer interface is easy to find in a gross way – just follow a data path outward from the computer's central processor until you stumble across a human being. Identifying its boundaries is a little more subtle. The key notion, perhaps, is that the user and computer engage in a communicative dialogue whose purpose is the accomplishment of some task'. With human to human interaction there is what John Morgan and Peter Welton (1986, p.108) establish as 'context, contact and code', the context describes the reason for the interaction which is normally transactional between humans and computer interfaces, contact is how the interaction is performed (point/click) and code is the agreed method of communication during interaction (text, compound icon and its lexicon). With the human to human model even if one of the participants is a novice using the code, understanding can still succeed, for example describing play during a cricket match, additional gesture will possibly inform the other respondent what has been implied, but more importantly both have a visual record of the event to inform comprehension. The user can visualise the event the central processor cannot. The central processor needs a specific command using an agreed written language to perform tasks. Of this Yukio Ota (1993, p.80) states that with natural written language 'the reader must have the same logic as the writer'.

Without an iconic interface the user must think in the logic of the central processor. The Hewlett-Packard Natural Language Project took one sentence query and produced 7000 variations of that sentence.[1] Although arguing for natural written language interfaces, Susan Brennan (1990, p.397) writes that these interfaces 'make the additional assumption that the sentences a user types will be well-formed. These will fail at anything that an eight-grade English student couldn't diagram'. With human–computer interaction this implies that the dialog has to be approximate for the user to be successful, but a precise language for the computer's central processor if it is to perform a task. Amorey Gethin and Erik Gunnemark (1996, p.17) state that 'languages are translations of "life", not other languages . . . they are direct "translations" of reality, of things, feelings, ideas, actions, of human experience'. Gethin and Gunnemark explain this further in an extensive endnote that there are 'simple proofs that we do not think in language,

[1] Research into command languages, database searching and so on. How shall I ask thee? Let me count the ways. The sentence query was, *programmers who work for department managers.*

but perhaps the simplest is to consider what we mean when we say we understand a piece of language, in the first place a piece, any piece, of our own language . . . We turn it inside our heads into something else that is not language at all. Let us call that something ideas, or pictures of reality' (ibid, p.24).

As described in Chapter 1 computer users no longer need to learn a complex computer language. A complete layer of Boolean logic has been hidden from the user and replaced by compound icons which represent what that program does. Desktop compound icons are underpinned with natural written language, programs that contain toolboxes and so on normally remove written language referents. However, it is noticeable that recent programs such as Macromedia Dreamweaver have returned natural language to toolbox palettes that contain compound icons.[2] For example, natural language which underpins the object toolbox palette such as Insert Table, Insert Image, Insert Applet and so on has natural written language visible on rollover. It is only when the meaning is clearly understood within programs that certain icons require no language. Originally, Internet pages were only possible through an understanding of HTML and more recently dynamic HTML, Java, Java Script and so on. Understanding of how to write in these languages has been slowly eroded. All page manipulation can now be created through a visual interface which allows the user to 'point and click' compound icons which write the appropriate script in background. In order to understand a program's functionality simple words associated to a computer compound icon are fundamental to an events understanding at the initial stages of learning, and at a later stage across language barriers. They help the user to understand what these pictures represent in their own minds.

In order to determine the level of meaningfulness of interface compound icons a questionnaire was devised to collect data that would measure the success or failure of one hundred icons, icon elements and symbols. As will be explained later in this chapter compound computer icons do not need to be precise in their reading, it is their overall understanding that is

[2] Macromedia Dreamweaver v.2.0, 1998.

important. The questionnaire was divided into four parts; 1) icons that are expected to function independently, with test subjects having a strong transactional interest in their understanding; 2) elements that make-up an icon or a complete compound icon which might have been learned through general computer use; 3) iconic gestures that have similar gestural meaning outside of computer interfaces; and 4) ISO/IEC symbols that has been determined by a governing body, and are normally used with no natural language attached. The questionnaire was completed by a group with similar interests and backgrounds so as to provide preliminary, but not conclusive data. It would also be important to state the reason why. Computer icons are normally developed by designers. In an interview Don Norman explains his point of view to Howard Rheingold (1990, p.10) that designers may think of themselves as typical users and therefore as part of an icons natural development, but 'after they have thought about the task for as long as you need to for proper design, they are no longer typical, they can no longer understand the average user: they know too much'.

Many application programs such as Adobe Photoshop, QuarkXPress and so on have an icon only toolbox. The functionality of each icon's meaning has to be explicit because a stand alone icon can be misunderstood, it is helped by the user's need to perform a task, and a lexicon which uses representative compound icons. For example when using Adobe Photoshop a photographer would understand the purpose of the crop tool, and graphic designers would understand what the pop-out text box tools imply which have been added to QuarkXPress 4 (see Chapter 6). As explained, the questionnaire was divided into four parts. The first section asked students from the Faculty of Arts University of Plymouth who used a computer and had photography as part of their study to recognise the function of the icons used in the Adobe Photoshop 3 toolbox (ten test subjects). All participants were made aware that the compound icons were from Adobe Photoshop. The Knife tool was given as an example, and all participants were then asked not to exceed two simple words as the answer. As

Recognition of General Icons and Elements.

100%

90%

100%

30%

10%

Recognition of ISO/IEC Symbols.

0%

100%

20%

will be explained later, computer compound icons are fluid in their translation. For example, the answer 'select area' to describe the Marquee tool is correct, framing is not (figure 1b).

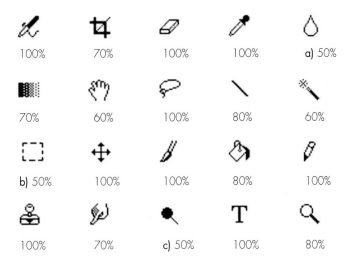

100%	70%	100%	100%	a) 50%
70%	60%	100%	80%	60%
b) 50%	100%	100%	80%	100%
100%	70%	c) 50%	100%	80%

Figure 1. Recognition of Adobe Photoshop 3 toolbox icons (10 test subjects).

A computer interface should allow users to recognise objects on the desktop so that associations can be made with all the possible choice of actions. Words and images used together allow users to 'rely on recognition, not recall; they shouldn't have to remember anything a computer already knows' (Apple, 1987, p.24). Human-computer interaction happens through an intuitive interface that iconically represents familiar objects found on the desktop. With no computer code language necessary to operate these systems ease of use encourages learning the meaning of an icon through play. The questionnaire was on paper and therefore icons could not explain themselves through play, and where recognition of function is poor, actual contact would place these icons into a context where meaning could be deduced (figures 1a, 1b and 1c, above). Pointing and selecting becomes inseparable from the desktop assumption that people are inquisitive, they learn the system because the environment appears accessible and engaging. To operate the computer users now look for familiar objects that suggest their function – language and description of functionality need only be approximate and not exact. In this way the interface allows the user to do real work for ordinary needs.

The *Apple Programmer's Introduction to the Apple IIGS* (1988, p.12) reminds the programmer of the importance of graphic consideration, returning their attention to the *Human Interface Guidelines: The Apple Desktop Interface* and states that 'objects on screens should be simple and clear, and they should have visual fidelity (that is, they should look like what they represent). Use familiar, concrete metaphors to represent aspects of computers and programs. The *desktop* is the primary metaphor in the Apple Desktop interface'. Ota (1993, p.78) believes that Isotype (International System Of TYpographic Picture Education) is the important 'roots of visual language' that interfaces now use. Central to the Isotype approach as to how picture writing should be constructed is the belief that images reduced to a common representation have greater effect than mere words – 'pictures make connections'. A combination of image refinement and Apple's assumption that people are inquisitive, aids intuition and creates a human-computer interface that is centred on users. However, Apple (1988, p.21) recognise that human activity is complex and that many factors are still unknown, but the major difference is the recognition that people want to achieve without the need to understand navigation through exact command-lines, 'specially at the first stage of getting new knowledge'. If any part of the two fundamental paradigms of recognition and action are not underpinned by visual metaphors and simple words interacting with computer interfaces will be reduced.

This is also supported by Evelyn Goldsmith (1984, p.30) who has undertaken extensive research into factors which effect images and their understanding. She writes of one experiment where test groups were given pictures only, text only, or pictures and text. Each group were given the same time limits during the experiment. Goldsmith writes that 'best performance was by groups given both pictures and text, with no difference between results from the single modes . . . on retest, all showed a significant drop in recall scores, but the pattern of results was similar, with the combination of pictures and text remaining the most effective'. Goldsmith's purpose was to test a hypothesis that images help in the main idea of a paragraph where images are used as illustration. The image can only aid the reader if it is visually concise in its message content and reflects the text. Therefore, an image might not help if the picture is merely decorative – it must have semantic values such as Isotype.

Partial Writing Systems

John Sören Pettersson (1996, p.51) cites the Hawaiian Sinologist John DeFrancis who devotes considerable time to 'dismissing the possibility of any extensive communication by means of iconographic devices', and goes on to point out that this is because the reading is not concise, but is this not precisely what is required of computer compound icons. Pettersson (ibid, p.55) concludes that to understand symbols 'we have to understand them in the medium in which they exist'. This is true of all sign systems be it for common use such as travel signs or specialist use such as electrical diagrams. Computers are becoming more common in their use, and specialist in their application, and all computer systems now share a common interface across different platforms (see Chapter 3). Computer users might have different aims and objectives for using computers, but they all share one thing in common. At the first level of system entry and in subsequent programs, be it for Macintosh or PC, the user interaction with a computer is the same, because they both use symbols and a natural written language which uses simple words.[3] All users engage with interfaces in the same way, but to achieve different tasks.

[3] This depends upon the individual design of programs, and if the interface guidelines have been fully implemented.

DeFrancis (1989, p.22-24) gives clarification to how language is used verbally and written in full, and how it can be described when specific descriptive words and visual representations are used together. First, partial writing, which is symbols combined with natural written language, and secondly, writing in full, which is natural written and spoken language. However, full natural written and spoken language can be riddled with metaphors such as 'the coast is clear', and 'time on our hands'. George Lakoff and Mark Johnson (1980, p.224) write that 'meaning is always a matter of what is meaningful and significant to a person. What an individual finds significant and what it means to him are matters of intuition, imagination, feeling, and individual experience. What something means to one individual can never be fully known or communicated to anyone else'. If partial writing is to work with visual metaphors then any accompanying language as DeFrancis describes must be specific, and must be free from metaphor or ambiguity.

Brenda Laurel credits Alan Kay as an 'interface hero', and the 'father of the personal computer'. Kay pioneered the use of icons instead of typed words for telling computers what to do next.[4] Many things came together that eventually led to the appeal of the Apple Lisa. The Xerox 8010 'Star' Information System preceeded Kay's SmallTalk which, according to Miller and Johnson (1996, p.70-76) demonstrated the 'power of graphical, bitmapped displays, mouse driven input, windows and simultaneous application', which is the most visible link between the Star and SmallTalk allowing users such as office proffesionals to 'produce, retrieve, distribute, and organise documentation, presentations, memos and reports'. This together with other influences on Kay (1990, p.191-207) as he himself states such as McLuhan, Piaget and Bruner who lead him to coin the phrase 'doing with images'. Lawrence Miller of the Aerospace Corporation and Jeff Johnson of Sun Microsystems describe the Star as the 'defacto standard of a good user-interface design'. However, it does not go unnoticed that successful interfaces owe much to what DeFrancis describes as partial writing systems such as Isotype. These many things that exist as state of consequence at a pivotal point in time creates what has now become the defacto standard which has other visible links that go back even further.

[4] At Xerox PARC (Palo Alto Research Centre) Alan Kay developed SmallTalk during the 1970s. It was a high level object-orientated programming language that could be used by non-programmers.

Man

Group (reproduced from Neurath).

Isotype

During the 1930s Otto Neurath had perceived Isotype as an instructional visual language with key basic words confirming the meaning. Ota (1993, p.95) cites Sanichi Shobo who says of Isotype that it is 'limited to transmitting the surface and general idea of words'. Symbols alone are insufficient because representational meaning can be misunderstood, until they have been learned. Marie Neurath describes Otto Neurath (1980, p.14) as a philosopher and educator who was the inventor of Isotype, but it was only possible to begin working on a picture language when the Government of Vienna 'gave birth to such an organisation in the form of the "Gesellschafts-und Wirtschaftsmuseum in Wien" in the year 1925 (which was in existence till 1934)'. Neurath saw it as a picture language system that makes selective statements and is not as a replacement for language (figure 2). However, Marie Neurath (1974 p.147) writes of Otto Neurath's concern for the symbol/word relationship and that it is important to understand what the symbol is there to achieve:

> There cannot be a "word by word" translation of a statement in the Isotype picture language into a word language; nor can a sentence in words be translated into a string of Isotype symbols. The Isotype representation of "a boy walking through a gate" is the symbol of a walking boy combined with the symbol of a gate; it is not a chain of symbols for: a, boy, walking, through, a, gate. The aim is to present some worthwhile information, show up some relationship or development in a striking manner, to arouse interest, direct the attention and present a visual argument which stimulates the onlooker to active participation.

Farming (sickle)   Industry (cog)   Trade (scales)

Figure 2. Isotype picture language (reproduced from Neurath).

Neurath saw the significance of using symbols with simple words that were unambiguous and teamed up with Ogden who had made a study of simple words. Together they combined Neurath's use of symbols and Ogdens choice of key words.[5] Ogdens Basic English (British American Scientific International Commercial) contained 850 core words such as open, paste, colour and so on which were mainly noun or verb. For computer interfaces these two fundamental paradigms of object and action are central to users completing tasks, and like Isotype/Basic each object on the computer desktop/window is named (Apple, 1987, p.24). The decision to publish an explanation of Isotype and a version underpinned by selective basic words is crucial to the system's understanding and adoption for other uses such as computer interfaces. In the same way as DeFrancis describes partial writing as symbols and keywords at airports and railway stations, the introduction of the 1980 facsimile International picture language/Internationale Bildersprache also includes the use of Isotype/Basic for traffic signs and so on. Neurath (1980, p.18) states that:

[5] Historical background is based on the recollections of Marie Neurath, which has been included in the editorial of the facsimile by Robin Kinross.

> A man coming into a strange country without knowledge of the language is uncertain where to get his ticket at the station or the harbour, where to put his boxes, how to make use of the telephone in the telephone box, where to go in the post office. But if he sees pictures by the side of strange words, they will put him on the right way (figures 3a and 3b).

Written words become redundant if users are unfamiliar with the language. Like Neurath's vision of Isotype words are needed to confirm what users are doing. Also, as Neurath has suggested, the symbols need to be the same between each country and changed to the natural written language of that country. A system where images are international, but more importantly consistently applied across visual language systems. This would allow users to become familiar with the symbols' meaning when the basic text is in their own language. This allows the user to associate what the denotation of a symbol is when in

another country if the written language is unfamiliar.
Therefore, users must be informed first as to the meaning of
compound computer icons through basic keywords and there-
after, by seeing the icon users will recall the meaning (figures
3c and 3d). Further assistance to meaning will also be achieved
if elements that make up the compound icon have a higher level
of denotation through consistent application in other visual
language systems, or by being a base element of semiotic communication such as arrow and box (figure 3a) (see Chapter 5).

a) Baggage Check-in
(reproduced from Neurath)

b) Baggage Claim   or

c) Baggage Check-in d) Baggage Claim
(reproduced from Dreyfuss).

Figure 3. a) and b) Neurath's 1936 version of the symbol for Baggage Check-in
and Claim, c) and d) from the 1972 Symbol Sourcebook.

Certain symbols elements can be combined with others to
expand meaning, which is also similar to the methods used by
the Maya to construct a hieroglyph from the same range of elements. Neurath describes putting signs together as the combination of Isotype and basic words, 'there is a sign for "shoe" (a
shoe) and there is a sign for a works (a building with a great
smoke-outlet). By joining these two words to make the new
word "shoeworks" we get the word for a works in which shoes
are produced' (ibid, p.50-52) (figure 4). Perception of the real
world changes, and images should change accordingly. For the
GUI basic words need to be considered first for all possible permutations before the accompanying compound computer icon
is created. This is what makes a partial writing system interchangeable with basic words in other languages, especially
within the GUI because the reason for interaction and how this
is performed has been decided for users.

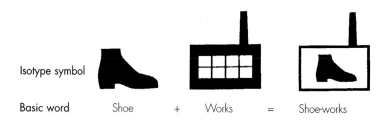

Figure 4. Putting signs together, the shoe is the root idea which has been infixed into the works symbol.

Ordinary writing within a partial system that is intended for the GUI will normally be action verbs such as new, open, close, quit and so on. Ogden stated that by cutting '250,000 words down to 850 and doing without its complex "verb"–system, Basic may well become a second language for all' (ibid, p.5). Robin Kinross points out that the constraints of an 850 word system leads to some 'awkward usages in Neurath's text. For example: "sign" is used where "symbol" would be more natural' (ibid, p.6). Ogden's Basic English might have been restrictive, but the principle applies to navigational signing systems and to the GUI. Here both sign and word are developed together, for example French airports have the same objectives as other airports and will have signs underpinned with entrée, sortie, arrivée, départ, and Spanish computers will have a simple word usage such as nuevo, abrir, cerrar and salir. Airports will use similar symbols to other airports, (figure 3, page 49) and computers will use similar compound icons to other computers (see Chapter 3). In this way Ogden's principle of Basic has become a natural development of the kind of simple words that should be used for partial communication within interfaces. Computer interfaces do precisely this – the same programs are used in many different countries, yet their interfaces remain identical except for the language of the country where the software has been distributed. Through utility the developer of the software have naturally standardised the compound icon being used – the same visual metaphor for all (figure 5).

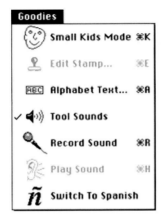

[6] Kidpix, v.1.2 1991, Craig Hickman and Brøderbund Software Inc.

Figure 5. English and Spanish interfaces of the same program (reproduced from Kidpix).[6]

To understand how the relationship between simple words and metaphors work it is important to consider what Gethin and Gunnemark have stated about how we think in pictures of reality, and how this relates to computer interfaces. In 1990 Thomas Erickson (1990, p.65) was part of the Apple Advanced Technology group. He stressed that metaphor is not a flowery language, but 'an integral part of our language and thought. It appears not only in poetry and novels, but in our everyday speech about common matters. Mostly we don't notice; the metaphor is such a constant part of our speech and thought that it is invisible'. What Erickson makes a case for is that metaphor is part of how we communicate, but should there be a distinction between how metaphor is used when words and symbols are expected to work together. This is not dissimilar to a mixed metaphor in speech, in which two or more metaphors are confused. Therefore, simple words and compound icons used together on the interface should ideally be both images that are metaphors, and simple words that are unambiguous

Many graphic communication systems such as Otto Achier's interchangeable body alphabet have evolved from the Isotype/Basic method, and this in turn can be recognised in the ISO/IEC 417 requirements for symbol design (see Chapter 4).

Rules by governing bodies might determine what symbols are acceptable. Visual language has a tendency to be governed by natural rather than forced developments. As Kress (1995, preface) has pointed out, there appears to be a return to hieroglyphs, and that users have brought about a natural development of emoticons through their desire to add further meaning to a message, (see Chapter 1) and also as Neuarth (1980, p.18) points out, 'words make division, pictures make connection'. Neurath understood the significance of combining word and image and he also took the view that symbols should be clear, work without words and be standardised.

Standardising Symbols

The precedent for standardisation had already been set out in 1909. John Foley (1993, p.222) writes that at the Convention of International Circulation of Motor Vehicles in Paris, 'nine European countries adopted a set of signs which were to become among the first internationally standardised symbols'. Ota (1993, p.44) cites a more recent example of an 'international organisation which is carrying out the standardisation of technology, quality control, and prevention of obstacles to trade through graphic symbols', it is also represented in 90 countries and has over 200 technical committees. Systems such as these publish guidelines for the use of graphic symbols on electrical appliances such as televisions, video recorders, dishwashers, medical equipment and so on (see figure 6, later). Unlike Isotype/Basic many of these symbols are not expected to be combined with natural language, they are expected to work on their own as Neurath suggests. Therefore, guidelines have been produced to ensure that new symbols conform to a symbol family standard. ISO/IEC rigorously enforce the standard and to enter a new symbol into the lexicon the symbol must follow the technical work procedures, and the methodology for the development of a symbol that conforms to international standards.

There are however safeguards that help in the selection of a symbol that conform to ISO standards. Harm Zwaga and Ronald Easterby (1978, p.282-283) have developed methods of

INFORMATION

ISO symbols (reproduced from Dreyfuss).

evaluating symbols, and more importantly a range of symbols with the same referent. For example, drinking water has 15 variants and information has 29 variants. For the comprehension and recognition of symbol variants Zwaga and Easterby state that the 'ISO evaluation procedure is to determine which one of a number of symbol variants for a referent is best comprehended by a sample of respondents representative of the user population'. For a symbol to be acceptable the ISO committee consider that 66% recognition is required. Representative symbols faired well, while abstract symbols were only understood if the respondent knew what it was that the symbol implied, if not then the response was 'don't know' (see Chapter 5). Zwaga and Easterby then go on to say that there is no absolute right or wrong response.

Even though a symbol has been standardised and entered into the lexicon, it does not mean that it will be understood. All test subjects identified fast run (figure 6a) mainly as fast forward followed by forward, move right and to right. The arrow of record review points in the same direction as fast run, however, surprisingly five test subjects did not attempt to give an answer, of those that did, the answer given was forward, repeat, back to start and return (figure 6b). The symbol for lightly soiled (figure 6c) applies to dishwashers, but has a stronger denotation as coffee shop, even in context it is difficult to interpret its true meaning as the relevant position of a selection switch. Most respondents wrote coffee, two wrote beverages. Adrian Frutiger (1991, p.348) states that this is one of the 'universally comprehensible' symbols which represents what it is. This symbol continues to be used, yet there was no recognition of its intended use, it can only be understood with a context because it is a coffee cup. The defibrillator equipment (figure 6d) has a specialist use, so the operator will have been taught the meaning of each symbol. Test subjects were not expected to identify what this symbol denotes, of those respondents that gave an answer most wrote man/elevator. Used in context this symbol will accompany two similar symbols. Each symbol suggests the weight of the patient to be treated; thin, the

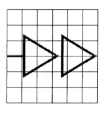 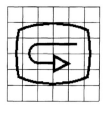  

a) Fast run
417-IEC-5108

b) Record review
417-IEC-5533

c) Lightly soiled
417-IEC-5296

d) Defibrillator equipment
417-IEC-5334

Figure 6. Symbols conforming to IEC Standard 147: Graphical Symbols (reproduced from ISO/IEC).

correct weight for size, or overweight. This is reflected in the size of the figure infixed within the compound.

The defibrillator is from a small family of symbols. Other ISO/IEC symbols are grouped together in larger families, and each reuses the same elements to imply meaning such as the 'on-screen' element. Unlike the coffee cup the reused main element is unlikely to have any other association. If the symbol uses familiar elements such as the 'on-screen' element that are used across a range of similar appliances such as televisions and computer monitors then users will understand that the infixed symbol elements imply the event that can happen on the screen. Ota (1993, p.148) writes that 'the relationship between form and form becomes much more important . . . the problem is syntax or how to appropriately express the meaning of the whole'. For example no test subject understood the meaning of the reference field (figure 7a), five out of ten test subjects understood arrow up and arrow down (figures 7b and 7c), while only three understood what the meaning of what two arrows facing each other implied (figure 7d). The infixed elements are all different, if the order of syntax was juxtaposed i.e. the infixed elements were larger than the 'on-screen' element then the symbols would be hard to understand as a family and possibly their meaning (see Chapter 1). Changing the order of syntax would not reflect how these functions naturally appear on screens.

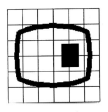
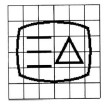
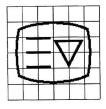
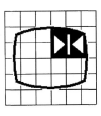

a) Reference field
417-IEC-5412

b) Page number up
417-IEC-5484

c) Page number down
417-IEC-5483

d) Picture in picture in freeze
417-IEC-5514

Figure 7. A family group of symbols where the user has only to learn
the meaning of screen once.

Base Lexical Icon Elements

Therefore symbols can fall into certain categories:

1) Easily Understood – regularly used and systematically applied across a range of appliances. Symbols that are unambiguous (figure 6a).

2) Partly understood – infrequently used, but containing base semiotic elements that are unambiguous (figure 7).

3) Conflicting – having a stronger denotation as something else (figure 6c).

The 'on-screen' element for monitors, television screens and so on are used across many visual language systems, and this is similar to the 'document' icon element which is also a base element of the computer compound icon lexicon because it is used among many programs. Arron Marcus (1984, p.365-378) was instrumental in the development of this element for the Xerox Star object-orientated interface design which appeared in 1981. Marcus writes that the 'Apple Lisa followed on the Star's approach', as a partial writing system that brought together understood and partly understood icon elements (figure 8) (see Chapters 3 and 4). As a base element the fundamental form of the document icon has change little since its original design for the Xerox Star. The document icon is therefore a common interface referent that will have other elements infixed. Common expressions are mainly understood, all respondents to the questionnaire correctly identified the document icon, elements infixed can then be individual events, their level of meaningfulness depends upon what transactional benefit that program has to users (figure 9).

All of the document icons on the next page communicate what their function is in some degree. For example, the denotation of the Text Encoding icon implies that the circular motion of two arrows surrounding the text is enclosing or encapsulating

55

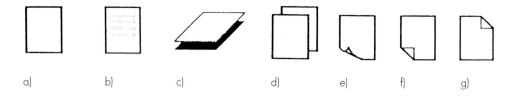

Figure 8. Development of the 'document' icon element. a) paper, b) with text added, c) isometric with a shadow for screen depth, d to f) further developmental stages, g) the final icon element for document (reproduced from Marcus).

Figure 9. The document icon is a base element of the computer icon lexicon.

the text in some form. Its meaning is still open to interpretation, whereas the Simple Text icon implies that only text has been generated here. Of all these compound icons it is the ISP settings document that is probably the most readable. Gesture or 'doing' with hands is described by Braffort (1997, p.17) as 'used to communicate information, in the same way as speech'. For example, David Stuart (1984, p.307) described the 'hand-scattering' Maya hieroglyph as one of the most common verbs. He also goes on to say that 'there has been a question as to what is being scattered or sprinkled'. Stuart does not question the hand gesture, he also writes that this is true of David Kelly before him that the elements being scattered remain unresolved, 'are these tiny circlets actually representations of a solid material such as corn grains or copal, or do they represent a liquid, such as water, or both? (figure 10)' The third part of the questionnaire discussed earlier asked the test subjects what in their opinion was the hand doing. Unlike the hieroglyphs which have the circlets in association to imply that the gesture is to scatter, it is only the first hand gesture from the questionnaire that has the hand 'doing'. Nine respondents identified writing or drawing (figure 11a). All other hand gestures need another element in association to imply direction or clicking, (figure 11b) picking up or dropping, (figure 11c) and releasing or grabbing (figure 11d). This section had the highest number of correct responses which was comparable to the first part of the questionnaire where the respondents were expected to understand what the compound icons denote (figure 1, page 42-43).

Figure 10. Examples of the 'hand-scattering' event. The circlets have now been identified as droplets of blood, the verb is sacrifice (reproduced from Stuart).

a) 90%   b) 90%   c) 70%   d) 80%

Figure 11. Gesture within the compound icon can increase readability.

The second section of the questionnaire contains elements which might have been encountered by the test subject. For text readability can be measured between complex and simple vocabulary. Once the method of forming individual letters into words has been mastered it is then the responsibility of the individual to obtain the level of competence that they require to communicate. Ota (1993, p.89) cites Rudolf Modley who wrote in the 1976 Glyphs Newsletter 24, that to learn a 'non-phonetic symbol, one needs to learn only the association between a visual symbol and what it stands for. In learning a phonetically spelled word, a child has to learn the graphic units associated with the phonemes, look at the word, say it, and then figure out what it means. Thus, for phonetically written languages, there are two steps – one from symbol to sound and another from sound to meaning. No such "two step" process is needed for symbols'. For a computer icon readability is achieved through previous encounters with elements that make-up the compound in contexts and as syntax through combination with other elements.

Conclusion

Users can visualise the event computers cannot. The central processor needs an exact command, therefore as the Hewlett-Packard research project suggests there are many ways to say the same thing. Compound icons do not need a precise interpratation to work, if as Gethin, Gunnemark and others have concluded that we think in pictures. The questionnaire gave some surprising results because the test subjects were visualising the compound icons in the context of the interface. Where icons are used without written natural language they are best understood because they share a common goal and code with what the Adobe Photoshop toolbox compound icons implies. Gestures that aid language such as the use of hands also did well to aid comprehension of an action. General icons that can be found on interfaces and ISO/IEC symbols did less well, test subjects were again trying to visualise the context. Only elements such as the document compound icon which forms part of base semiotic communication, which can be found throughout interfaces were recognised by all. When integrated with other elements the combination aided syntax. For most compound icons a prompt is required to help the icon explain what it denotes. Pictures do make connections with tasks and work well with simple words. Maya hieroglyphs have phonetic elements within the lexicon, which are less noticable because all elements are visual. This combination of representation and precise phoneticism leaves the reader in no doubt as to what the writer intends. Interface icons that are metaphors which represent nouns or verbs in the real world should be underpined by simple natural language that is unambigous, as there is a transactional nature between humans and computers, as Dom Norman states, 'people and tasks come first, interfaces come second' (Rheingold, 1990, p.7).

Designing Icons for the Graphical User Interface

By analysing what would be appropriate for designing computer compound icons it must be recognised that different medium such as a computer interface will require different considerations that are applied to established modes of communication such as paper-based design. The unique quality of interfaces is that the same graphic element can appear in different forms according to the platform or browser viewing it. This is true of colour, complex web scripts and browers which can dramatically change the viewing size of a web page, therefore for the original designer, objects on interfaces can be viewed in a way that was not originally intended. These options need to be considered and it needs to be recoignised that control of this is limited. In order to establish what those design possibilities are, computer icons can be gauged against other elements of design, how they are used, and what their design criteria is. Websites might possibly contain icons which are greater than a 32 x 32 pixel matrix, but in order to establish some form of standard system icons are used. Magazines can direct the reader around the page by creating a positive reading order. Conflict, contrast or harmony can alter the reading order between icon elements without altering their physical size, and optical rather than mathematical centres decide the balance of elements used in any design. This chapter explores what design rules carry over from established graphic design principles, to the Graphical User Interface. Importantly, we look at what elements of computer iconography have become successful and have evolved to be reused to make new computer compound icons that reinforce what these icon elements denote.

Bill Buxton (1990, p.12) believes that the Macintosh was a victim of its own success, 'the best ideas are the most dangerous, because they take hold and are hardest to change. Hence the Macintosh is dangerous to the progress of user interfaces precisely because it was so well done! Designers seem to be viewing it as a measure of success rather than as a point of departure'. With little challenge the design principles of the Macintosh interface have been adopted by other computer operating systems. Ben Shneiderman (1990, p.358) writes that Microsoft and Hewlett-Packard went to great lengths to copy the Macintosh 'Look and Feel' (United States District Court, Northern District of California. Plaintiff, Apple Computer, Inc., vs. Microsoft Corp. & Hewlett-Packard Co., Defendants, April 1992). Whereas there were many alternative solutions, 'the similarity of Windows 2.03 and Windows 3.0 to the Macintosh is the result of designer's choices and not because of necessity. Many design alternatives exist that would provide equivalent function'. Also there are many ways to have 'improved on the function of the Macintosh and to have created a visually distinct appearance'.

It seems unfair that one corporation appears to infringe upon the intellectual property rights of another. Copyright can be successfully argued for other works such as books, pictures and so on. However, it can also be argued that the visual elements that make-up the Graphical User Interface are units of meaning, and to deny access to such a computer language reduces the chances of one language for all. Upon reflection it maybe a good thing that the court ruled in favour of Microsoft Corp. & Hewlett-Packard Co. (although it may not have appeared so at the time). Apple lost their monopoly, allowing Microsoft to standardise the visual language system developed by Apple, and in doing so, influenced the development of many different computer platforms allowing users to interact with computers and each other through computers. So, we now have a system that has standardised a 32 x 32 pixel matrix across many computer platforms. What are the design possibilities and limitations for even the simplest element that make up

Figure 1. A selection of Artillion icons.

the compound icon? The computer icons original conception came about through the recognition by computer software and engineering researchers at Xerox PARC that a different approach to how people interact with computers was needed. Alan Kay (1998) has confirmed that the icons for the Apple user interface were designed by graphic designers, but that the prototype version of that interface was designed by him and his research group at Xerox PARC.

Ben Shneiderman (1998) goes further and says that 'graphic designers are good partners in the design process, but often people with little graphic skill or thought wind up inventing icons'. Writing phonetically is open to all that can write, if icons are a visual language should this not be so for them. As William Bull (1998), a computer science graduate with a flare for the visual makes clear, 'I've taken one art class, Art100, and a huge number of math and computer science classes'. What Bull goes on to say is that 'if you figure that we've got the basics of clipping, fast blitting and double buffering hands down it's no wonder that moving a window or a view around in real time is becoming more common. Unfortunately once we've overcome the programming challenge the need for aesthetics kicks in' (figure 1). Like the grammar for any language there are rules to aesthetics that can alter our perception of an image, but unlike grammar they are not enforceable, they are merely guidelines.

Visual Reading Order within a Compound Icon

Richard Gregory (1970, p.18-19) writes that psychologists in the early part of the 20th century used dot patterns to investigate perceptual organisation, and how even an array of random dots can form 'configurations'. In the same way as Gestalt psychologists considered primary stages in perception it is important at this point to also consider the fundamental relationship between elements within the compound icon which can influence syntax through proximity and size to each other. To explain this it is easier to consider the analogy of the number ten in a pack of playing cards. The only difference in this analogy is that the playing cards are square. The square contains ten individual items, but because there is an order to the arrangement a pattern is formed. Likewise these ten elements can appear as two groups of five, or two lines of four and so on, the mind forms relationships. If the ten items are scattered at random the pattern changes, elements that are close and appear organised merge to form other relationships and so on (figure 2). This can then be extended to consider the possibilities of proximity for more complex shapes. According to Clive Chizlett (1999) this is a phenomenon of perception that 'relates to the incorrigible habit, incorrigible drive, to signify. Thus simulacra are observed: a dressing-gown on a door-hook is seen as a monk with his cowl up; a twin-rooted parsnip is seen as a manikin. If one is disabled from understanding a given icon, one assigns it a meaning which would normally baffle the icon's designer'.

Adrian Frutiger (1991, p.17) states that 'there is no element of chance around us, but that all things, both mind and matter, follow an ordered pattern . . . From the recognition of this fact we draw the paradoxical conclusion that the production of an ordered form is easier than making of a disorder, a *nonform*'. The visual reading of the organisation of an icon takes place in the mind through the eye (Gestalt meaning 'form', German School of Psychology. Their Laws of organisation were discussed in a paper by Max Wertheimer in 1923 entitled Principles of Perceptual Organisation). Frutiger (ibid, p.16) goes further and cites Albert Einstein as having said 'words or speech, written or spoken, do not appear to play any part at all in the mechanism of my thought processes. The basic psychic elements of thought are certain signs and more or less clear pictures, which can be reproduced and combined "to order"'. If the mind organises shapes into ordered patterns, it therefore stabilises form by creating imaginary links between elements by connecting the line of least visual resistance. The psychological perception of these visual connections appear to be strongest on the horizontal and vertical axis followed by the diagonal as described by Frutiger's (ibid, p.18-20) simple test of memory and sign. In this test the

Figure 2. Elements and their relationship to each other.

Figure 3. Imaginary visual links between elements.

mind perceives a common link although one does not physically exist, and therefore establishes a relationship. This can be demonstrated through the analogy of the number three playing card. Here there is a strong axial line which exists down the centre. At this point there are no distinguishing features between the elements, they are simply aligned (figure 3). Of this Keith Albran and Jenny Miall-Smith (1977, p.38) write that 'what is generally meant by a psychological response is that in which the viewer brings to the percept information which is additional to the process . . . information which is not physically available'.

By continuing to use the playing card analogy, if one element is altered either through colour or size the relationship of the elements also change the reading order of the content of the compound icon. The three elements (figure 3) at the same size have no definite starting point other than the user's custom of reading order. Supposition can be problematic if the reading order assumption is left to right and from top to bottom. Henry Dreyfuss (1972, p.76) pointed out that:

In South Africa, most of the men who work in the mines are illiterate. The miners, therefore, are given instructions and warnings in the form of symbols rather than words.

In an effort to enlist the miners' help in keeping the mine tracks clear of rock, the South African Chamber of Mines posted this pictorial message:

But the campaign failed miserably. More and more rocks blocked the tracks.

The reason was soon discovered. Miners were indeed reading the message, but from right to left. They obligingly dumped their rocks on the tracks.

How users percieve information, or establish what a reading order possibly is should not be left to assumption, as the order of reading priority could be different to what is expected. Also, interface icons do not perform an icon by icon narrative similar to the example illustrated by Dreyfuss. They do however form part of a dialogue between the computer and the user as examined in detail in further chapters, and as already shown in Chapter 1, individual Maya hieroglyphs can say many things within one compound, as can computer compound icons. Maya hieroglyphs have an internal reading order because it is a language with grammatical rules. Computer icons rely upon a reading order which is visual in its order of priority. This suggests that visual priority is part of a syntax if the compound icon is to be successful. At this point by continuing to use the playing card analogy and increase the size of the element at the bottom, the user's eye will generally prioritise that element (figure 4a). The user is drawn by size regardless of custom. If the intensity of the hue of one element amongst the ten is altered the user is attracted through colouration (more on this later) (figure 4b). If a second square element is altered to the same hue the user's attention is halved and so on (figure 4c).

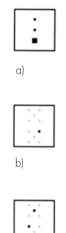

a)

b)

c)

Figure 4. Establishing a reading order within a compound icon.

Conflict, Contrast or Harmony within a Compound Icon

At this point it is important to recognise that these techniques are regularly used by magazine designers. The scale might seem overpowering to make any form of meaningful comparison to computer compound icons, as computer icons might seem overly large when compared to letters that are 10pt in body size of a volume of magazine text. What the magazine is trying to achieve in its overall layout is not differnt to individual letters, in this respect both are applicable to compound icons. The reader is subconsciously directed around the page through the designer's understanding of visual reading order through either contrast or harmony, but never conflict. In the sense of design for paper, an example of conflict would be the use of two typographic families from the same group, used on the page together – the page would lack adequate visual variation and conflict because neither typefaces are sufficiently different.[1] With the Dreyfuss example, the illustrations harmonise, there is no variation, so the viewer is left to choose their own reading order, left, right or centre. With positive contrast the reader can be directed to view a picture on the right hand page first, and then to the top of the left page to read the heading of the article. The eye can then be directed towards the article by a further element positioned at the beginning of the main body of the text, such as a drop cap (large initial letter). This draws the reader around the page and into the subject, layer by layer. Obviously an icon is very small in comparison to a magazine double page spread, but it should have a positive reading priority. To compare an icon to graphic design page layout principles it is important to establish what page design principles offer, and what are the fundamental shifts required when we move away from paper and towards the screen. Paper will have either:

Conflict, no visual definition between the page elements.
Harmony, little definition with an agreeable use of page elements.
Contrast, high definition with a positive difference between the page elements.

Page design is further complicated by the fact that there are four basic elements of design – headings, body text, images and white space. Each element can contain many items within, with the exception of white space. Colour is important but is not a basic element, any good design should also work well as either black, grey or white (known as page colour). What this means is that the four basic elements can be manipulated to either merge or standout. It is this organisation of elements that determines what the message order is. So therefore, the basic elements can be altered through colouration to make the page either conflicting, harmonious or contrasting. With computer icons the distinction between what is conflicting and harmonious is less obvious, what is obvious is a contrasting arrangement. In the example of the Macintosh 'Assistant' icon, the greyness of the assistant element places emphasis on the item that it is offering to assist with (figure 5a, 5b and 5c). If greater emphasis is given to the 'Assistant' the arrangement becomes harmonious, they are still different, but equal (figure 5d and 5e). If the colouration of both 'Assistant' and item become indistinguishable then the arrangement becomes conflicting (figure 5f). Unlike the magazine double page spread, it becomes difficult to differentiate between what is harmonious and what is conflicting for a computer icon. If computer icons are to be considered as visual language, then contrast aids syntax.

The blackness or greyness of the page can be determined through the choice of elements and how they are used. Contrast will give the elements a positive reading order. However, elements used to design a paper page can be reproduced at very high resolutions, in comparison computer screens view at very low resolutions. Images in print can therefore have fine details and sharp curving lines even though the pixels are within a square matrix. Computer screens are normally 72 dots per-line-inch whereas print can have a matrix of 2,540 dots per-line-inch or higher. High resolution print can also allow for a degree of control over a page, for example using a selection from an extensive family range of typographic fonts (more on this later) can alter the overall greyness density of the page. The computer screen has to compensate for this by making shapes appear smoother than they actually are by anti-aliasing the pixels (adding grey or intermediate colour pixels around the image edge), but being clumsier without the level of control that paper can achieve. Steve Gibson (1999) has been researching sub-pixel font rendering technology for Microsoft and considers that 'out of sheer desperation, a technique known as "anti-aliasing" was developed. It attempts to employ shades of gray where font designers would like to show only "part" of a pixel. The hope is that our eyes will tend to average two adjacent gray pixels to see one in the middle'. Gibson goes further and states that a pixel is 'actually composed of three "sub-pixels": one red, one green, and one blue. Taken together this sub-pixel trippled makes up what we've traditionally though of

a)

b)

c)

d)

e)

f)

Figure 5. Conflict, contrast and harmony.

[2] Sub-pixel rendering technology is a part of the Microsoft clear type reseach program. Unfortunatley at present this technology only works with LCD and not CRT.

[3] The monitor has an intensity to voltage ratio which means that every pixel has an intensity equal to x. For an uncorrected PC this means x $\wedge 2.5$.

as a single pixel'.[2] However, until sub-pixel rendering is fully developed colouration to alter the relationship of elements within an icon can only be achieved through the adjustment of the saturation of hue and its lightness or brightness giving screen elements some degree of fine single pixel control.

Even though colour is not considered a basic element of design, it is an important consideration when designing for screen display, especially the Internet. It is accepted that a web safe colour palette contains 216 colours, yet these colours will appear wildly different across a range of computers because of the monitor gamut. The next problem is the inconsistency between all the monitor gamma responses of different computer systems. Macintosh systems normally have a built-in gamma hardware correction which is set to $\wedge 1.4$ and an output signal of $\wedge 1.8$. PCs have no correction with an output signal of $\wedge 2.5$[3] but can have a graphics card installed to correct the problem. Therefore, an image that appears correct on a Macintosh will appear dark on a PC, and vica versa, and an image prepared on a PC will appear 'washed out' on a Macintosh. The next problem is that most users own and view the web through a PC. Macintoshes tend to be a graphic design studio tool which is used for designing for print, where correct colour is important. To publish on the Internet it is important to use colours that the majority of browsers use.

Philip Greenspun (1998) writes on his website that 'your graphic designer might have worked really hard using Photoshop to get a particular shade of yellow into a graphic but there is no way for Photoshop to encode in a GIF or JPEG file what shade of yellow the designer was actually seeing on the monitor'. Robert Berger (1998) of Carnegie Mellon University gives a further example of what can happen between systems, 'if a color having a red element of 50% and a green element of 25% is displayed on a CRT with a gamma of $\wedge 2.5$ without correcting for gamma, the resulting intensities will be 18% red and 3% green. In addition to being darkened, the color has been shifted toward red. Dark red fleshtones are a common manifestation of failing to correct for CRT gamma.' The reason for this is that 8 bit colour that has been indexed to 216 results in 6 x 6 x 6 distinct colours which are made up of combinations of 00, 33, 66, 99, CC and FF for red, green and blue. For the web the Macintosh gamma response point can be altered to reduce the colour shift with the installation of a gamma control panel (included with Photoshop 3 and upwards). This panel allows for a compromise between the two systems by allowing the user to change the gamma from ^1.4 to ^2.2. Altering the gamma can create a large shift in appearing colour. This is still below ^2.5 and is still a compromise known as the 'web average gamma', but it is still the best way of avoiding 'dark red fleshtones' (1998).

The reading order of a compound icon can be dramatically altered through the use of colour without changing the size of the elements (figure 6). This is an important factor for computer icons as size is at a premium, and the fact that icons are normally image only. With paper major elements become primary information (everything you need to know about a story before it is actually read), and the story itself becomes secondary information. Positive primary information such as sub-headings, headings, and images leave the reader in no doubt where the eye should go. Therefore the reading order can be determined by, adjusting the size of an element, and the saturation of hue and its lightness or darkness against other elements. In the earlier example (figure 4) the size of the elements which make up the 'Assistant' icon are the same (figures 4c, 4d and 4f). Their only difference is the colouration of the elements which alter the relationship. Elements which work at one level of saturation/lightness or brightness become overpowering or understated when altered. Therefore, what influences the reading order of a compound icon is:

Icon Elements +	Icon Colouration =	Icon States which:
Size and shape in	Saturation of hue and	Conflict
relation to other	its lightness or	Harmonise
elements	brightness	Contrast

Figure 6. Primary influences of the reading order of icon elements.

Using Space within a Compound Icon

Gitta Salomon (1990, p.270) of the Apple Advanced Technology group states that 'we need to take great care in applying color. We cannot choose colors in isolation; they must be chosen in context. Our color "compositions" may need refinement and alteration with the addition of every color. If a specific color scheme is important, we have to protect it from colors that could alter its appearance. For instance, Shell Oil Company placed its yellow shell-shaped logo on a controlled red background. They realized the logo's impact could be severely reduced by leaving the background to chance'. The question of isolating elements from their background was raised by Carl Dair (1967, p.91) who describes the use of a border through the analogy of a pigsty, 'This is very effective in keeping what's inside, inside, and keeping what's outside where it belongs. Typographically, its called a border'. Obviously Dair was describing design for print, but his observation also holds true for icons, as the border forms a relationship with the elements contained within. Unlike print the appearance of the media can be altered by the user. Desktop patterns and colours provide the user with the opportunity to customise, and change the overall colour of the compound icon. Borders as such are not necessary, but edge definition helps to distinguish what belongs inside the compound icon and lessen the effect of what surrounds the icon (figure 7).

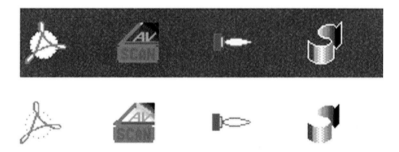

Figure 7. Icons and their relationship to the background.

At present a 32 x 32 pixel matrix keeps elements within an icon together. If the matrix is increased which is entirely legitimate to analyse as more and more individuals develop their own website then, the internal relationships that work closely together extend the possibilities for the relationships that elements can form within a compound icon. With increased matrix size it is important to revisit magazines to analysis how negative space (white space) is used. White space actually means more than the head, foot, foredge and back margins of a publication. With a magazine space can be considered at different levels, there is space between letters, words, lines and paragraphs. These blocks of text interplay with other elements of the design, space then becomes an issue between headings, sub-headings, images and so on. These relationships are not finally resolved until all the elements have been brought together. If elements within an icon are considered as squares, and four squares are placed close together a fifth negative white space is created between the four squares in the form of a thin white cross (figure 8a). Visual oscillation occurs when both positive and negative space are balanced. The eye perceives both four black squares and a thick white cross (figure 8b). Any more space and the squares become four individual items (figure 8c). Space now serves to break-up the relationships. If the squares were on paper and the page edges are added this also changes the relationship of the squares (figures 8d, 8e and 8f).

Computer icons do not have edges as such, but they either do, or do not, have a border between itself and the rest of the desktop. In the example of a compound icon with a border (figures 8d, 8e and 8f) when there is more white space between the group and the border (figure 8d) the elements still function as a group. The square elements relate to each other even when the border is removed (figure 8a). When the edge has been added the relationship of the elements become closer with the border (figures 8e and 8f) and these elements are no longer related to each other. So, it is not only what surrounds an icon which impacts upon it, it is also the compound icon itself. The relationships illustrated above do not take into account that

a)

b)

c)

d)

e)

f)

Figure 8. Negative and positive space between four equal elements.

a)

b)

c)

d)

e)

f)

Figure 9. Different icon boarders as metaphors, repeated use helps to indicate family type.

when a border is used, it is also normally part of the metaphor. The most commonly used metaphor for a border is a file. (figure 9a, 9b and 9c). Other borders create family groups of icons such as extension (figure 9d), control panels (figure 9e) and control strips (figure 9d). Regardless of what a border represents, shapes can be assigned meaning, which allows the user to identify the compound icon family type and function.

So, borders establish a relationship with the content of the icon. Returning to page design and the layout of elements for print, elements within can either have a symmetrical arrangement or an asymmetrical arrangement. Normally the arrangement is asymmetrical throughout from the initial page architecture to the smallest elements of any page, the crossbars (horizontal strokes) of uppercase and lowercase characters are always above the mathematical centres while the serifs on opposite sides of a letter are often not exact mirror images. Paul Luna (1992, p.19) considers that 'introducing controlled irregularities into a typeface' could stimulate the reader's eye when lines of type are being continuously scanned. Asymmetrical has always been preferable if only by millimetres for the architecture and fractions of a point for type because variation in what the eye perceives keeps the mind of the reader alert. Most publications use a serif typeface for the main body of text for this reason. With paper any element placed on the page at the mathematical centre optically appears to be below the centre, being pulled downwards. If the element is adjusted by the eye to appear central (optical centre), mathematically the element will be above the central position. Again, because of the inability of the screen to render fine detail, and the fact that a serif typeface is used over a large volume of body text the real question is between a dynamic asymmetrical or static symmetrical use of elements within the compound icon (figure 10).

The example on the next page (figure 10a) illustrates the representation of text being placed higher within the icon rather than lower. If the text was placed lower within the compound icon it would given the appearance of visually falling forward (figure 10b). When the icon is mathematically divided (figure 10c) and a block of 4 pixels are placed at the mathematical centre, the point appears to be falling downward (figure 10d). If the block is moved upwards by one pixel the point appears to be more central (figure 10e). With 32 x 32 pixels the position of a centre point using a single pixel can only be above the central line, or 17 pixels high, and offset either left or right. The dimensions of the matrix create a natural tendency to be asymmetrical when using a single pixel (figure 11a). However, 4 pixels can sit around the mathematical centre (figure 11b).

a)

b)

c)

d)

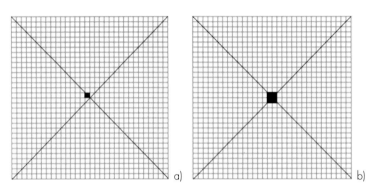

a)   b)

Figure 11. One pixel can only be asymmetrical.

e)

Figure 10. The mathematical and optical centres of an icon. e) appears to be more central than d).

Applying this to the icons in figure 12 demonstrates that this already happens within icon design. All icons are from the control panel family. The Map (figure 12a), Startup Disk icons (figure 12c) all appear to be centred and balanced on the horizontal for both the slider and the content image. However, when the mathematical line for the centre is added both sliders are two pixels above centre and both Map and Disk are one pixel above the centre (figures 12b and 12d). The final Keyboard icons main content is well above the central line while the slider is one pixel further to the left appearing central because of the shadow that gives depth (figures 12e and 12f).

All elements appear balanced against each other within the compound icon, but this is based on optical correction not mathematical calculation. The control panel icons (figures 13a to 13d) have all been adjusted upwards by one pixel, the

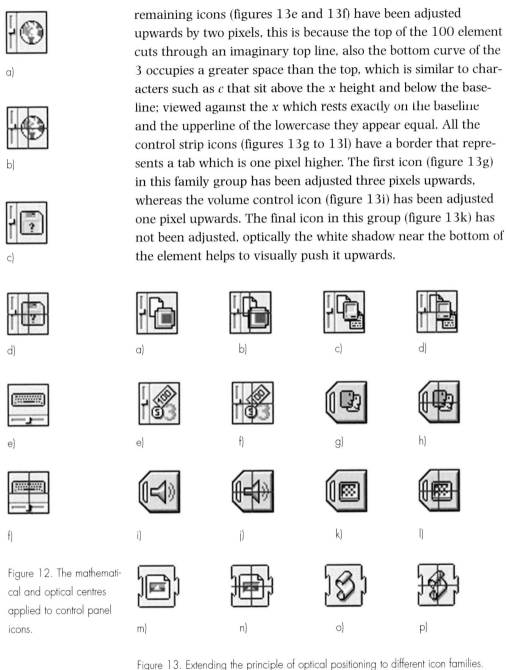

remaining icons (figures 13e and 13f) have been adjusted upwards by two pixels, this is because the top of the 100 element cuts through an imaginary top line, also the bottom curve of the 3 occupies a greater space than the top, which is similar to characters such as *c* that sit above the *x* height and below the baseline; viewed against the *x* which rests exactly on the baseline and the upperline of the lowercase they appear equal. All the control strip icons (figures 13g to 13l) have a border that represents a tab which is one pixel higher. The first icon (figure 13g) in this family group has been adjusted three pixels upwards, whereas the volume control icon (figure 13i) has been adjusted one pixel upwards. The final icon in this group (figure 13k) has not been adjusted, optically the white shadow near the bottom of the element helps to visually push it upwards.

a)

b)

c)

d)

e)

f)

Figure 12. The mathematical and optical centres applied to control panel icons.

a)

b)

c)

d)

e)

f)

g)

h)

i)

j)

k)

l)

m)

n)

o)

p)

Figure 13. Extending the principle of optical positioning to different icon families.

Finally the extension family icons (figures 13m to 13r) use a jigsaw piece metaphor as a border. The features of the boarder that represent the jigsaw parts are unequal, the first two icons (figures 13m and 13o) have these features off centre by one pixel upwards of the left and one pixel downwards on the right. The remaining icon (figure 13q) also has the same off centre arrangement, by one pixel to the right at the bottom and one pixel to the left at the top. The use of elements within each icon then depends on the shape and use of lightness or brightness of the objects that are represented. The first icon (figure 13n) has been positioned exactly in the middle, what helps to visually force it upwards apart from the folded right hand corner is the top lighting and shadow between the slide case and the transparency itself. The second icon (figure 13p) has been adjusted upwards by one pixel, the lightest part of the shadow is one pixel further from the centre, optically this balances the scroll element.

Using Type within a Compound Icon

It has already been stated that computer icons are normally image only. There are however many specific actions relating to text. This is the nature of what a computer is used for. The letterform of the Roman alphabet is an optical art and not an exact science based on mathematical positioning. Both the serif and sans serif can be traced back to the chiselled inscriptions found on the Roman monuments such as the Trajan column. The characteristic of the serif can be attributed to the tools which inscribed the letters onto the stone. This combination gave the final inscription the shape of letters that we recognise, that is, 'stressed' strokes of different thicknesses. In 1910 Frederic Goudy was one among many who was influenced by the letterform qualities of these inscriptions. By returning to base source Goudy was able to use the past to inform typography for the future. All good typeface design looks back, recognises the qualities and places this into an appropriate context for the present. Digital typography should be no different, it is merely another kind of medium (McLean, 1995, p.86-90).

For single word recognition sans serif families have more choice and the ability to add further expression through typographic stylisation. Sans serif typefaces normally have an equal mono-line weight throughout with squared features. For example, single san serif words have greater legibility, and Edward Johnston's san serif was designed for use on the London Underground in 1916 and was based on the old style script of the Roman inscriptions, the thick and thin strokes were given an even weight and the serifs were removed (figure 14). The face was an ideal adaption of the past for the London underground, where large single words needed to be clearly recognised against other competing styles of typography used in advertising (Sassoon, 1993, p.124). This does not discount the use of serif characters within an icon, but because of the fine strokes of serif faces under a certain size the subtle nuance that forms the characteristic of a type family can be lost.

JOHNSTON

Figure 14. Edward Johnston's alphabet for the London Underground.

In order to understand these differences it is important to look closely at the optical structure of a typeface, and the decisions around its construction. Newspapers, journals, traffic sign systems and car manufacturers have produced their own versions. Monotype Times New Roman was developed for *The Times* in 1932 and is probably one of the most successful typefaces of this century, therefore Stanley Morisons' campaign for typographic reforms for *The Times* serves as a good example. Before Morison English newspapers were mostly set in modern faces. These faces tended to be of a fine typographic construction, reflecting the style that worked for the slower printing speeds of the previous technology. Printing machine speeds and volume of print were increasingly leaving the final newspaper impressions of these modern faces grey or squashed. Morison had made the connection and understood the problem of using type in the wrong technological context. His solution was to use modern features which retained the legibility of an old style face, and by doing so, regain the clarity of impression that had been lost. The alteration of the typographic features of many typefaces such as Baskerville, Perpetua and Plantin were tested (Carter, 1987, p.88-95).

It was a revised Plantin which was finally used by Morison. The redesigned family became Times New Roman restoring both the aesthetic and legible qualities suitable for machine composition. Morison also had to consider technical limitations, such as 'ink-spread'. With movable type each size had to be physically manufactured. Optical adjustments were made for the size differences of body text and display type. Creating a digital version of a typeface is through informed interpretation and not as a faithful copy of the original. Therefore, typography has always adapted when technology has changed. Digital typography has evolved to meet the demands of new technology, yet it is not only a change of technology, but also one of medium. Digital fonts are not physical, software generates the font as either an outline for the printer or as a bitmap for the screen. Within computer compound icons, type is a screen bitmap and not an outline algorithm.

There is a potential pixel resolution difference between a monitor and the printed output. Viewing elements such as type in print and on-screen is different, what is seen on a screen is not necessarily what is achieved in print. A comfortable viewing size for a screen is normally 12pt yet this does depend on the appearing size of the typeface. Although typefaces optically sit on the same baseline, the x height, ascenders and descenders can have different weights and sizes. Photina has a tall x height whereas Bembo has a smaller x height making one appear larger than the other when they are both at the same point size. For example two typefaces, 11pt Bembo regular has 51 characters and 11pt Photina regular has 49 characters across a column measure of 20 picas, yet both are serif typefaces. The computer needs to know 'set-widths' and also their 'side-bearings', which determine how letters fit with each other inside a word. The computer does not measure the line of type in point sizes but divides the characters up into 'set' post-script fractions. This allows the font to form other relationships with characters and spaces in the formation of words which have been predetermined by the foundry. It is also altered by the type management settings, that can preserve character shapes and place on-screen characters against each other with precision, and whether or not the bitmap has been anti-alised. So, it is a question of personal judgement by eye (for that computer and monitor) whether type displayed on-screen will work (figure 15).

Photina in 12pt   Photina in 12pt Bembo in 12pt
Bembo in 12pt
a)   b)

Figure 15. The appearing size of type on the body can make a family seem large or small.

The practical outcome of this is that serif typefaces tend to reduce less well, and have to be used in larger sizes to compensate for the 'stressed' thick and thin strokes that suffer when anti-alised. Sans serif typefaces normally have an equal mono-line weight throughout, with squared features that survive reduction to approximately 11pt depending on the appearing size of that family. Amongst these families, each has its own characteristics giving that family a personality, and it is also best to remember that typefaces are not intrinsically legible. Phonetic alphabets take a considerable amount of learning, once learnt their shapes can be used to add personality. The simplest example is a typeface such as a sans serif. In a heavy weight would be appropriate for fast food. It would be even more appropriate if the letterform was rounded and not squared off as a sans serif. Letterform creates meaning through associations, the high street signs advertising and so on subliminally educate in their associated meaning, and the elegance of a serif typeface would be inappropriate in this case. This can be taken further, everything about the design of the McDonalds 'M' which has squared off features and curves simply wants the customer in and out as fast as possible, quite literally fast food (figure 16). It is also interesting to note that symbols.com point out that the 'M' represents 'fire' in alchemy (1998) .

 *fast food*

Figure 16. The typography suggests that McDonalds would like a fast turn around of customers, serif faces are a different typographic class and would not convey the same message (reproduced from MacDonalds).

Users have learned to associate meaning with the shape of letterform, therefore there is a typographic class structure with an associated connotation that is powerful because users are normally unaware of its message potential. Typefaces and their fonts that form part of an icon or their associated banners influence the way a user reacts. Because there are over ten thousand fonts which make up two thousand families there are only a few families which continue to develop for each change in technology. Baruch Gorkin and Tom Carnase have researched type families that have made the transition through the technologies and have concluded that of these many thousand, it is only 50 that form a typographical core of what has been designed well (Gorkin and Carnase, 1995, p.IX-XVIII). Any radical alterations that do not conform to what a user typographically expects not only reduces legibility, but also credibility. Programs like Photoshop manipulate images, and will probably have text capacity. Unlike programs that are designed to use type for print such as QuarkXPress, imaging programs are bitmaps that do not require font 'hinting' (instructions to reduce the arbitrary 'in' and 'out' of pixels within the matrix).

a) Canon logo

b) Plug-in

c) Kern edit

d) Postscript

e) Type Reunion

f) Information

Figure 17. Characters and their related actions.

They still would benefit from 'side-bearing' and 'pair-kerning' certain letters which require a special relationship to fit well together, such as Ye Yo Yp Yq and so on (A well designed font will set side-bearing values, which have an optical equivalent of give-and-take or 'wrenching' this is because after learning to read users recognise the shape that a word makes, therefore awkward gaps in words impair legibility. There are also some pairs of characters which require a special 'pair-kerned' relationship).

The overall relationship of the possible pairs of letter fits would be more appropriate for other parts of a web page that use text generated from image bitmap programs. Within a compound icon text is normally a single character such as a logo that can be associated with a range of applications from one manufacture (figure 17a), a short word describing the action of the icon such as the Adobe Photoshop plug-in which gives the program additional functionality such as special effects, filters and so on (figure 17b). The Kern edit program allows the user to adjust the predefined pair kern edit tables established by the font manufacturer for page make-up programs that support algorithms. The type within the compound icon describes what the application program actually does (figure 17c). The following icon (figure 17d) not only uses type as an identity with the manufacturer, but also, it is a single character that represents one function over a range of different Postscript printer fonts. Unlike TrueType fonts, PostScript fonts are divided into two parts – the printer font algorithm needed by the output device, and the bitmap font needed by the screen. The next icon, Type Reunion has a character within the compound icon to represent type families being grouped together in a sub-menu from the font pull-down menu (figure 17e). Type Reunion will only place the PostScript font family in the sub-menu. The final icon, MacOS Information Centre contains tips and links to websites so that users can obtain the most from their computer (figure 17f). According to Frutiger (1991, p.348) there are 'universally comprehensible' signs, and there are also 'universally comprehensible characters' such as 'i' for information and so on.

Reusing an Icon Element within a Compound

Otto Neurath (1980, p.27) considers that a 'picture which makes good use of the system gives all the important facts in the statement it is picturing. At the first look you see the most important points, at the second, the less important points, at the third, the details, at the fourth, nothing more'. This similar to the Maya hieroglyphic system which could prefix, infix and postfix many elements into a glyph compound. Unlike Maya hieroglyphs computer icons stand alone and are not cross referencing each other, although there are similarities for both systems especially in the way in which elements have been joined together to form new computer icons or glyphs. With Maya glyphs joined elements can be recognised throughout a text and between texts and places. Tom and Carolyn Jones (1995, p.94-2) point out that 'women are sometimes identified with no more than an emblem glyph in which this same na-head has displaced the usual *k'ul* prefix, such as to prescribe the reading, *na*-[site name]-*'ahaw*, especially in cases where the woman is from a neighbouring site and an important political or military relationship is assumed'. Even though the female na-head is phonetic, it is still recognisable as a female head (figure 18). Computer iconography has evolved rapidly to reuse parts of visual elements which have taken on meaning (figure 19). The hand has come to represent a 'doing' (verb) function which is then joined with an object that represents an application program. As pointed out during Chapter 1, a verb does something to an object with the subject of the verb. It therefore informs the user that they can 'write' with this program, and what it is that they can 'write'. Figure 19 demonstrates that for computer users the hand element represents an application program that they can be 'doing with something'. There are only two elements – the hand and an object. The second element then informs the user what that something is.

Cancuen   Dos Pilas   Man

Tikal   Site Q   Yaxchilan

[4] Lady Katun Ahaw retains the Piedras Negras [site name] and not Man [site name] in the Stele 3 text.

Figure 18. Female head glyph (phonetic na) joined with [site name]-'ahaw (reproduced from Jones and Jones).[4]

Figure 19. Hand with pen (verb) describing a 'doing' relationship with various application programs.

Figure 20. Three ways to write man according to the space that is available (reproduced from Chizlett).

By reusing successful elements the learning of either the Maya hieroglyphic or computer icon lexicon can be reduced. Many other systems do precisely this, for example Clive Chizlett (1999, exhibit 4) writes that the Chinese concept-script 'pictograph for human and man is a primary or radical character on its own. Naturally the concept human has its semantic function to fulfil within many hundreds of the compound ideographs'. The Chinese mark that represents man can change its size and scale to fit the many combinations that it is likely to be used within the compound (figure 20). This is similar to Maya hieroglyphs because the compound can contain many elements where phonetic values might be required to avoid ambiguity. Computer icons rely upon visual syntax therefore more elements will create ambiguity. The questionnaire of computer icons used during Chapter 2 contained 100 icons and elements, and none exceeded four elements within the compound icon.

John Morgan and Peter Welton (1986, p.9-10) summarised Wilbur Schramm's model of what two parties need when communicating. Schramm's model implies that both 'sender and receiver have to share the same set of skills: they have to use the same language or code, and they have to use words or signs in the same way. For this to happen, they must have experience of the same social system and culture'. The Schramm model can be graphically expressed and applied to the example on the previous page when using icon elements that have taken on meaning, and because of other successful combinations that meaning is strengthed further. For example, the *na*-[site name]-*'ahaw* glyphs the decoder knows that it is a female while second glyph element will tell from where. Circle A represents familiar/unfamiliar elements. Circle B represents the combined compound. Area AB represents what is familiar to both through systematic application to other compound icons or glyphs (figure 21). In the computer icon 'writing hand' and Maya *na*-head illustrated on the previous page (figure 18 and 19), many different elements from A can be joined with AB to create new icons or glyphs. It is a lady but from where? (figure 21a) It is an application but of what? (figure 21b)

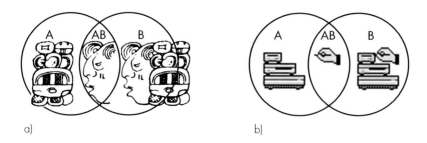

a)   b)

Figure 21. Schramm model applied to and hieroglyphic and computer icons elements to form compounds.

Maya glyphs work together as narrative and their reading order is verb, object and then subject. Although this chapter has already stated that the reading order for computer compound icons will depend upon visual factors of contrast, harmony and so on, the Schramm model above implies that familiar and frequently used elements might not be first in the viewing order, but are first in the reading order because they form part of a core lexicon. Also, computer icon elements normally serve a 'doing' purpose where many of the verb functions are described by similar elements such as hands, pens and so on. Of this Jakob Ossner (1990, p.14) writes that 'by conventionality we mean that a community of senders uses one particular representamen'. This understanding of what the core lexicon elements represent by predomenantly being the same object that is represented helps to inform the viewer what the other elements might possibly be.

Conclusion

A 32 x 32 pixel matrix has limitations, yet the unquestioning standardisation of the matrix and other parts of the Graphical User Interface actually assist in the understanding of the metaphors used. Therefore, with a fixed matrix it must be decided which factors impact upon the design of computer compound icons. Many approaches can be taken to investigate how the conventions of graphic design for contempory magazines which are grounded in the constructivist approach of the 20th century can be applied to computer compound icons. Therefore the reading order of magazine pages and the relationships between page elements can possibly inform icon design, if these rules hold true for a compound icon. Icon elements can be arranged in order of size and shape in relation to each other within the compound, and this in turn is influenced by the icon's colouration through saturation, hue and lightness or brightness of these elements. By making alterations to these points it will determine the icons' state of either being conflicting, harmonious or contrasting. However, magazine page layouts can can have many subtle nuances that do not apply to icons therefore reading orders are only effectively established when elements within the compound icon are contrasting. Also, some form of border is generally used, either as part of the overall metaphor which helps to build a family identity and is a further clue to its function, or simply as a border helps to distinguish what belongs inside the compound icon, and lessen the effect of what surrounds the compound icon.

Successful compound icons also retain the fundamentals of what makes good graphic design using an asymmetrical arrangement to stimulate the eye, and therefore being less tiring to look at which is similar to magazine spreads and how letterform is constructed. Also, optical and not mathematical centres are used to position elements within the compound icon, forcing the eye up yet appearing central, which again helps to stimulate the user's eye. With 32 x 32 pixels the position of a single pixel centre point can only be asymmetrically offset either above or below, left or right. Visual perception organises shapes into some form of meaningful wholeness, therefore the completed icons themselves are also less confusing if they do not exceed four elements, and that these elements should already have an established meaning whenever possible. It also aids understanding if the element has been visually averaged to represent that category of item by consciously selecting features that are common to several variations of the same object. However, unlike print it is apparent from the Schramm model that visual reading order, or selection of order through viewing size is different for the reading order of computer icons. If the notation attention of the largest element within the compound icon is not understood it might be viewed first, but it is frequently-used elements that might be second in the viewing order that inform the latter if they have been learned through the use of other compound icons or other systems outside of computer interfaces if the implied meaning is the same.

Computer Compound Icons and their Families

This chapter builds upon the previous chapter which considered the visual qualities that computer compound icons should have to aid syntax. To understand how syntax can be better understood the development of a symbol is explained through a corporate identity programme, and how it should be used throughout a large organisation. Corporate identities which have calculated how it should be applied and what graphic element should be used to imply meaning are explained in two case studies. Therefore, this chapter not only places emphasis on optical construction, spatial harmony and contrast, but also explores the denotation and the connotation of elements used within a compound symbol. Each case study uses phonetic alphabet elements in the final design, and each has visually considered the overall connotation that would best represent that business. This will then be extended to include the graphic requirements for a family of symbols, after the traditional method of symbol design has been explained to demonstrate how elements form relationships with each other. Finally these traditional methods will be used as a point of departure for computer compound icons, and to establish the strengths and weaknesses of a 32 x 32 pixel matrix, and also how corporate websites interpret icon design when considering the overall 'mood' of their websites.

The factors that influence our ability to reason such as emotion, philosophy and ideology are taken into consideration when designing a graphic symbol. Many choices are normally subliminal through being part of the culture that the symbol is created by, and for. These factors will be different depending upon culture. Consider the Maya culture that has developed independently of 'old world' values. In the Maya hieroglyphic writing of the 'new world', Eric Thompson (1972, p.51) writes that the heart element within the compound glyph represents human sacrifice. Today in many cultures the heart represents love as depicted on Valentine cards and in the use of metaphorical speech, a person 'looses their heart' or their feelings come 'straight from the heart' (figures 1a, 1b and 1c). Even western cultures that share much can surprise, for example the heart symbols original use in Sweden was a toilet and still means defecation (1998). The heart on a Valentine card has been made into a rounded soft form, whereas the Maya heart element was drawn with complete details including the connecting aorta (figures 1d, 1e and 1f). Our culture is the framework in which we reason, it will colour our philosophy and govern our understanding towards what is being denoted.

In the illustration right the first two symbols are used in connection with medical websites (figure 1a and 1b). The first symbol is on a medical society homepage entitled 'Straight from the Heart' (1998) (figure 1a). The second symbol can be found on any American website that is a member of the American Heart Association (1998) (figure 1b). The next symbol (relative link button) is from an American on-line dating agency (1998) (figure 1c). The heart has primarily stayed the same for all three, the only exceptions are the elements that have been infixed into the heart symbol. The shape of the heart has been accepted and reapplied to different categories of use, such as welfare or love. According to symbols.com 'It is an anarchistic graph that has yet to find a place in any conventional sign system. Nonetheless it is well known throughout the Western world as a sign for togetherness or love'. Graphically it is related to Aries and means union. As pointed out earlier, the Maya use of the heart infixed element is different, but its shape and form for what it represents remains consistent when used in different hieroglyphic arrangements (figures 1d, 1e and 1f, above). What Thompson (1972, p.51) says of this is that 'this idea could be expressed placing the head of the bat alongside the heart or the bat may appear alone but with details of the heart glyph

a)

b)

c)

d)

e)

f)

Figure 1. Different cultural representations of the heart.

infixed. The reason for this combination is that the vampire bat, so common in the Maya lowlands, draws blood from its victims and is thus an excellent symbol for sacrifice' (figure 1e).

All the examples on the previous page exist because of cultural isolation from each other at some point or degree. So, if a common culture was shared through computer networks then objects and their actions should be familiar to all. Before user interfaces were standardised by the actions of Microsoft, multi-functional computer platforms were equipped with several types of Graphical User Interface. These interfaces ranged from numerical and text data to still/moving graphic images and sound. Koi Kobayashi (1986, p.120) recognised that through these mixed media human reasoning has to interface with a machine, and that everyday activities such as banking, shopping and so on, will be through such a machine. Many such activities as described by Kobayashi are now common through access to the Internet. Computer users and owners of digital television can now shop from home, internet users instantly change from being a shopper, to interacting with other cultures on any subject. What something means in one culture can be alien to another, but this appears to be less obvious with the Internet where the iconography of many websites share the same denotation with many cultures. Douglas Schuler (1996, p.35) believes that culture is the 'thread running through society that removes people from their everyday existence while simultaneously placing them in the universality of everyday existence'. Web development tools and browser software are normally the same regardless of country, and as pointed out by Bill Buxton (see Chapter 3) the design of user interfaces go unchallenged. By accepting something as a standard gives a consistency to computer compound icons and helps in their recognition, but also creates a common culture.

Consistent Use of Symbols

A consistent use of symbols helps an image to be recognised for what it represents, for example systematic application of a symbol through a corporate identity programme helps the symbol to be identified with a certain idea or concept and company. Wally Olins (1989, p.7) believes that to be effective 'every organisation needs a clear sense of purpose that people within it understand. They also need a strong sense of belonging'. Therefore, the purpose of any corporate identity scheme is to convey a message about a company both internally and externally. The identity becomes not only an organisation's unifying focus, but also a means of saying what it is that that organisation does, and therefore designed to give the viewer an idea of what they can expect. These symbols are reinforced with the organisation's name. The typeface itself is again selected to confirm the idea and endorse the message. It is the overall connotation of the symbol that sends the message, the viewer is not expected to disassemble the elements of the design and read the message like a sentence. In the same way as computer icons work, it is the wholeness of the design that puts across the overall message. This message can then be applied to unify and identify all the parts that make up an organisation. It is at this point important to identify what makes a symbol work within a corporate identity, and from this what is applicable to computer compound icons.

Symbols are normally made of graphically reduced elements brought together as one image and organised to imply meaning. A corporate identity manual takes this further and is compiled to ensure that all parts of a large organisation implement the identity in unison, therefore all parts send the same message which increases the recognition of the symbol. When designing a symbol using the traditional methodologies of the drawing board the designer constructs an architecture based on the grid. When the grid is removed the elements that make up the design retain a spatial integrity that holds the whole symbol together. Design integration across a corporate range had

a)

b)

Figure 2. Paper matrix
and computer icon matrix.

[1] Chicago, Burlington &
Quincy Railroad Co.
(CB&Q); Northern Pacific
Railway Co. (NP); Great
Northern Railway Co.
(GN); and the Spokane,
Portland and Seattle
Railway Co. (SP&S).

already been identified by David Carter in 1976. By this time enough corporate identity user manuals had been designed for him to produce one of the first books on this subject. Carter's (1976, section 2) book of different identity manuals is evidence that a grid architecture and systematic application was an established practice amongst corporate designers by using a paper matrix. This matrix was used to develop and deploy a symbol, and is not dissimilar to a computer icon's matrix (figures 2a and 2b). The only difference is that symbols used as corporate identities are not restricted to the size of the computer icon matrix (figure 2a).

As Carter makes clear, with this practice established, many large organisations sought to use and benefit from a single image that could unite an organisation (figure 2a). On 2 March 1970 four railway companies merged to form Burlington Northern (1999).[1] The Chairman, John Budd, and the President, Louis Menk, wrote a joint letter to the company employees stating 'this program is more than a mere system of design and set standards. It is also an expression of confidence and pride in the capabilities of the new Burlington Northern and its men and women who will ensure its success' (Carter, 1976, section 2). As Olins (1989, p.148) makes clear, both the Chairman and President of Burlington Northern are addressing the primary purpose of identity, 'the organisation wants to present itself as clear and comprehensible. It wants its different parts to relate to each other so that people can find their way around its divisions, companies and brands. Applied systematically across all four railroad companies, the aim of the symbol was to unify its members and project an outward image to the world that all these companies were now one. All were railroad companies and the symbol could have been an abstract device expressing values or qualities, yet the solution was to use italicised letterform within the logo to imply motion, and a bold font weight to imply strength. If any one of their activities was singly identified this would alienate the other parts of the organisation and defeat the primary purpose. Activities that are focused in one direction, such as the car mechanic, seamstress and so on can be represented directly by that activity. Like sole traders computer compound icons normally perform one action, and can therefore be representative of what they do.

The designer must consider different qualities for the symbol because it will probably be applied to different media. Corporate design has to contemplate the obvious letterhead, glossy brochures, and sides of vehicles through to the sides of cardboard boxes. Each application might have a different surface texture, and even a different hue, saturation, lightness or brightness to balance colour between lighting conditions for ink, paint and so on (metamerism). The symbol used on computers can now be included in the designer's range, adding transmitted light to the breadth of possible applications. This is where computer icons differ, they are not corporate identities, and do not normally need to consider other media in their design. Icon design does however, need to consider how other computer icons have been designed as a family. To reduce any confusion between a symbol and an icon Aaron Marcus (1984, p.365-378) states that 'an icon is something that looks like what it means; it is representational and easy to understand'. C. Marlin Brown (1999, p.87) considers that a 'symbol is a sign that may be completely arbitrary in appearance; we must learn the association of its appearance with its meaning'. Computer icons use representation to denote meaning, while the symbol can be abstract, the connotation of a symbol is acquired through learning.

Case Studies

The two case studies that follow examine the design methodology used for creating a symbol. The first case study investigates the development of the symbol by drawing reference from the Roman alphabet and graphic representation, the second was developed from a primary source, the Maya culture of the classic period. Both were constructed using a grid architecture on a computer and not on a drawing board. The 32 x 32 pixel matrix was not considered an option at the time of the development of these symbols.

Case Study 1: Marine Security Limited

The business of Marine Security Limited is the security of marine craft, and marine related activities such as the transportation of craft between United Kingdom ports and overseas ports. The organisation also has other related activities and do not necessarily concentrate on a single output, for example only guarding boats. To be precise and obvious within the design of this symbol would cause the alienation of other parts of the company's activities. This is especially important if the business aims of the organisation are those of expansion, but only in marine related and security associated areas. Letterform is an obvious choice for inclusion in this kind of symbol because it avoids being exact about any one area of the organisation. However, because marine activities are the common linking basis of the business, water and how it is represented can be used. Thomas Erickson (1990, p.12) writes that 'traditional approaches to creative design require playfulness and produce new ideas via inspiration'. Water is a basic graphic element, any form of 'playfulness' or more appropriately, manipulation to achieve visual equalisation of elements and reading order through contrast of size is used – wavy lines are wavy lines and the element referent will probably retain its semantic value for most people.

In the final design of the symbol (figure 3) a circle which is graphic base element, allows the three other elements to form a relationship of proximity to each other, and the reversal of the circle allows the elements to be viewed reversed out of a solid background. The 'M' (Adobe, Eras Bold) is underlined by the connotation of water stepped and repeated to denote movement and a gradient fill has been added to create the illusion of depth. It is also based upon the most commonly used signs for water. Rosemary Sassoon and Albertine Gaur (1997, p.20) state that wavy lines have 'persisted throughout history, indeed the Egyptian hieroglyph for "water" was written in this way'. Symbols.com point out that 'it appears both in modern ideographs, as an alchemical sign and as an ancient Greek sign for water'. The wavy line can also be found to represent water-course, water surface and the sea – in the Japanese art of warfare many wavy lines together represent the sea and so on (1998). The 'S' is drawn in freeform as a representation of an estuary, breaking out of the circle. The shape suggests 'S' but only works as a representation of an estuary by the context in which it has been placed (see figure 7, page 94).

After the decision has been taken as to the role of design elements, abstract and so on, visual equalisation and reading order will give the symbol semantic implications, and this is through manipulation within a grid architecture. It is at this point that certain graphic elements can be tested and eliminated according to the overall connotation of what the symbol will finally denote. The type that accompanies the symbol retains its own spatial integrity, also like computer compound icons the letterform that accompanies the symbol should not compete for the user's attention. It is simply in a typeface that will be used throughout the company to help the symbol unify all parts of the organisation. The grid is not being used to slot the elements neatly into boxes or flush with each other along the grid lines, it is there to aid visual alignment as the relationships are not mathematical but optical (see Chapter 3). While both type and symbol are being compiled within the grid it is important to note that physically the circle sits proud of the left side grid line of type. When the grid is removed the company name and the symbol appear optically aligned. This is also true of any typographic construction, characters like *r* sit on the baseline whereas the *c* sits below the baseline and above the *x* height, optically both appear the same height – this is no difference from the relationship of elements within the symbol (figure 4).

Marine Security Limit

Fleet Mill Lane
Any Town
County
United Kingdom
Post Code

Telephone
Fax

Figure 3. Final symbol
with type on letterhead.

Figure 4. Optical character balance of the baseline and x height.

The First Element: Background Circle

The circle is the unifying element, the other three elements within the design have to create a visual tension with each other if a contrasting arrangement is to be achieved. A computer-generated grid is placed over the circle, so that spatial integrity and size differences can be tested between the elements that will form syntax. The use of scale helps in the emphasis of the reading order. The 'S' is largest element, it stands for security, but it also has the connotation of the estuary implied through the basic graphic of the circle where the positive and negative relationship between both allow space to flow through the 'S'. This element has now created an additional shape due to the law of proximity to its right side, having been formed by what has been covered by the 'S' and the remaining edge of the circle. This additional shape has no syntactic value, however it could create an additional appearing element that might detract or imply something else (see Chapter 3).

The Second Element: M

Not only was the type family Eras chosen for its range of mono-line weights (monolines can be subdivided further into even and uneven width monolines), it was also used because the visual characteristics of the type family help the words project authority. The font family contains six weights, Light, Book, Medium, Demi, Bold and Ultra Bold (figure 5). The range of font weights allow any design to be firm or gentle but always projecting a feeling of strength. Family completeness and range will also aid legibility because this family is a sans serif and similar to transportation signs and so on (see Chapter 3). Capital letters have more authority, whereas upper and lowercase still gives authority especially in the bolder weights of this family, but is less aggressive. By using the same family throughout the typography will harmonise well together, but also add contrast to any printed material when the range of weights are diverse, such as Bold for headings and Book for the main body of the texts used in forms and so on. The family is then applied throughout all business communication and publications. The use of the 'M' in the logo helps its association with the company as part of their identity because unlike the 'S' it is Eras.

Marine Security, Eras Light
Marine Security, Eras Book
Marine Security, Eras Medium
Marine Security, Eras Demi
Marine Security, Eras Bold
Marine Security, Eras Ultra

Figure 5. Eras, sans serif typeface family.

The Third Element: Underlining the M

To bring attention to a letter or word a line underneath can be sufficient, or the line can be an additional element giving that referent within the symbol further meaning. It has already been pointed out that the symbol for water can be traced back to cultures with different writing systems right back to pre-sumarian cuneiform signs. There is nothing new in wavy lines, merely how their pragmatic use influences how they appear. Here a graphic representation of water stepped and repeated to imply movement through a gradient fill that also creates the illusion of depth. The referent element is designed to appear as blue through to white whenever colour is used. L. De Grandis (1986) describes blue (darker hues) as a suitable signal colour because of the spectral sensitivity of the human eye in failing light conditions, and would therefore be suitable for the sides of marine craft. The relationship between the company name underneath the logo is one that does not detract from the other and this is also true of colour, used once it focuses the attention of the viewer, if another colour is added to the symbol the impact is halved. All other elements of the symbol are designed to be white within the blue background of the circle.

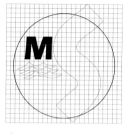

a)

b)

Figure 7 Figure 7. a) Symbol as basic design elements. b) Optically balanced with elements reversed white out of the background circle. c) As a final symbol. d) Spatial relationship with the company name, note alignment of company name with symbol breaking across the line. e) Applied to stationery where the symbol and type have a spatial relationship with the paper and its edges.

c)

d)

e)

The Fourth Element: S

The visual equalisation of elements, but not reading order, lead to the conclusion that the 'S' should be based upon a monoline width referent to Eras that could have a further connotive value if draw as a freeform shape. The shape must still retain its recognisable features as letterform if further meaning is to be implied. During the developmental process several even widths were experimented with so that the reading order would not be overpowering or understated. The final 'S' is drawn as a free-hand graphic but retains the sans serif characteristic with a consistent line weight, a serif would be inappropriate because its characteristics would not fit with the overall 'mood' of the symbol. The final 'S' has been elongated to break the circle at two points. The apex of the letter completely breaks the circle, the baseline partly breaks the bottom of the circle. This partial break at the bottom is to anchor the 'S' to the background, and stop it visually 'floating' within the confines of the design. When considering this element against other elements within the symbol visual syntax is aided not only through contrast of size but also contrast of elements. The 'S' is abstract of what it represents while the gradient fill of the wavy line is illustrative.

Changing a characteristic of a letter is often used by the designer to change the meaning or add emphasis. The second example also changes the letterform to imply a cultural connection, but in order to do this the change needs to be radical and like the 'S' of Marine Security will loose the subtle nuance that is typography when changed to a symbol. If a symbol needs to 'bridge a gap' between two cultures then a designer from the other culture would through intuition think and work accordingly. Adrian Frutiger, although Swiss, had lived and worked in France for some time before he was asked by the chief architect Paul Andreu to design an alphabet for Charles de Gaulle airport. Frutiger (Signals, Channel 4) believes that there is a 'Frenchness' to the sign system he designed through the typographic features he added to the font by giving the 'l' a tail which distinguishes it from his other type designs such as

Univers or Futura. Also, to reflect the airport itself, of this Frutiger (1980, p.80) says 'that the first considerations were of a purely geometrical nature, such as the balancing of the round letters with the circular plan of the building'.

Case Study 2: Print and Publish Belize

The original brief for Print and Publish Belize was the redesign for the Belizean Government Printing and Publishing imprint for the newly formed Belizean Publishing. What makes the design retain its Central American characteristics are not dissimilar to Charles de Gaulle airport where Frutiger has given consideration to architectural features specific to location by giving the alphabet a unique personality. The design for Belize is based upon Maya carvings at Xunantunich 'The Maiden of the Rock', which is in the Peten lowlands of Belize (Figure 10b, page 98). The requirement and rationale for the symbol was that it had to embody a national identity particular to the region and the authoritative nature of publishing and of print in Belize (the government printer is required to oversee the printing of voting papers, this is written into the Belizean constitution). The implicit connotation within the symbol had to express the aspirations of Government printing outside of Belize to an international audience that it was modern (figure 8).

To some degree the main design work that was carried out in Belmopan, which is the administrative capital of Belize also requires the consideration of many elements of cultures and their environments to inform the symbols connotation (which are different) between cultures. The original design for the Government Printer uses the central image of the national flag to promote Belizean identity, in the final design it is retained for reasons of political ownership, and therefore to insiders and outsiders the Government Printer is part of a greater association. The emblem is therefore used on all government publications to aid national identity and internal communications. In its new role it continues to undertake the same function and gives authority to the new symbol. When the emblem is placed outside a Belizean cultural context it is simply an emblem,

PRINT
BELIZE

NO 1 POWER LANE
BELMOPAN
BELIZE   CA

FAX 501-08-23367
TEL 08-22127
OR   22293

Figure 8. Symbol with type on a letterhead. The word Print can be substituted with Publish.

Figure 9. Emblem of Belize.

whereas the symbol would in Belize simply be a symbol until what it denotes through association with the emblem is recognised (figure 9). Outside of Belize the overall connotation of the symbol implies print (repeating elements around a cylinder), design (through modernism and the clean lines of 20th century sans serif), Central America (by reflecting elements of Maya architecture), and because of this there is still a Belizeaness about the symbol.

There is an influence over this region that is distinctly Mayan, none more so than drinking Belizean beer from a bottle with its temple logo, while being sat in San Ignazio and seeing the top of Xunantunich towering through the rain forest many miles towards the border with Guatemala. The local population is made up mainly from people with an African or Spanish descendancy, but nobody can fail to miss the significance of the colour green through the Maya culture and how this permeates through Belizean society. Choice of colour can be subjective with cultural factors influencing the choice. With Belize certain colours have stronger associations with political parties because of the general standards of literacy (election ballot papers use colour to aid choice). Green is acceptable as a warning colour on hurricane posters, red is a political colour and cannot be used by the government printer as it has a stronger connotation with a political party. There are Maya (2 million), but the majority come and go throughout the region with little regard to national boundaries. The final symbol for Print and Publish Belize does not attempt to express itself as Maya writing, because the writing system is too explicit for the purpose of this symbol. After photographing Xunantunich it was decided that repeat patterns within Classic Maya architecture was the appropriate approach (figures 10a and 10b, page 98).

Changing a Letterform into a Symbol Element

In figure 10c (I) Helvetica upper case was chosen for its optically consistent line weight. It was then horizontally scaled 155% to reflect the proportion of the Maya carving in figure 10a (II).[2] The letterform was then converted into paths, with

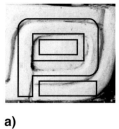

a)

b)

c)

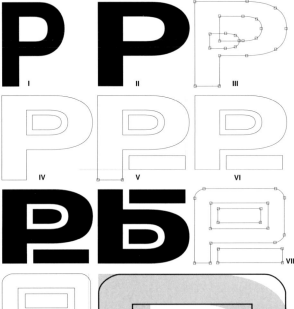

Figure 10. a) Symbol
element superimposed
over Maya carving.
b) Print and Publish Belize
symbol source, Maya
carvings at Xunantunich.
c) Changing typographic
characters into symbol elements by undermining the
subtle curves used in the
original typeface.

the elements split within the path, so the central bowl outline of the 'p' could be cloned (III). The cloned bowl was reduced in proportion and then extended horizontally, so that the centre appeared optically consistent (IV). The bar would be in close proximity to the neighbouring elements within the final symbol, therefore the bar below the 'p' was drawn as a freeform graphic with an optical weight equivalent to the upper and lower bowl (V). The right side of the bar is also shorter than the 'p', yet both appear optically on the same vertical alignment. The ascender has been reduced in length so that the bar and ascender both sit on the baseline. The final outline has had the paths joined and grouped (VI). The final element was filled and cloned, the duplicated element was rotated 180° and then rotated around a reflection axis to create the mirrored element 'b' (VII). The final elements were placed within a grid structure. Each 'pb' element within the paper grid was vertically reduced to signify the reproductive nature of printing and publishing. This was the test point for the first version.

The initial design was first developed to adapt the Maya designs of their Classic period to Roman letterform. This approach was to help the symbol make the connection between two cultures. It soon became apparent that using the letterform as it was typographically designed to be used was not working, and was therefore abandoned after the responses of test subjects to different modes of visualisation were evaluated before (VII) and then after (VIII). Upon reflection, by removing the subtle nuance of the letterform and giving it an overall abruptness the shape for the counters and ascenders were taking on an overall Mesoamerican mood. This break with established typographic form was now building the elements into a compound symbol. Its western 'mood' comes from what survives this process which was similar to how the 'S' in Marine Security was developed. Also how the 'p' as an element was grouped together with the other elements to form the overall symbol, and finally the choice of typography to underpin the symbol. Therefore, what has survived this interpretation is the methodology used for the architecture of the symbol through the visual alignments on the horizontal grid line. The bar below the 'p' and above the 'b' have been physically foreshortened to appear optically correct and so on (figure 10c, page 98). The addition of the bar to the 'pb' of Print/Publish Belize makes the symbol more in keeping with its Central American theme, while retaining a simplified monoline connection with the sans serif letterform. The overall connotation of this identity is to retain its Mesoamerican mood, yet have a western appeal.

Changing from a typographic form to symbol (VIII) required the 'p' to be converted back to paths, certain points were removed and line segment characteristics were altered from curves to straight lines (figure 11). The curve of the 'p' has been reduced with the addition of straight line segments, the position of the bar was considered so that the right vertical alignment of the 'p' is still optically correct (IX). To establish which line segments and points were altered, the Roman letterform was used as a template (X). At this stage the final element went through the same process as the initial Roman letterform when applied to the paper grid (XI) (figure 12). The final symbol was then tested across a range of limited applications to ensure that it would be optically pleasing on a range of surfaces and scales. Having done all of this, and to ensure that semantic implications for the symbol exist, if the final symbol is not also asetichically pleasing then it will fail to be believable and therefore unconvincing to anyone.

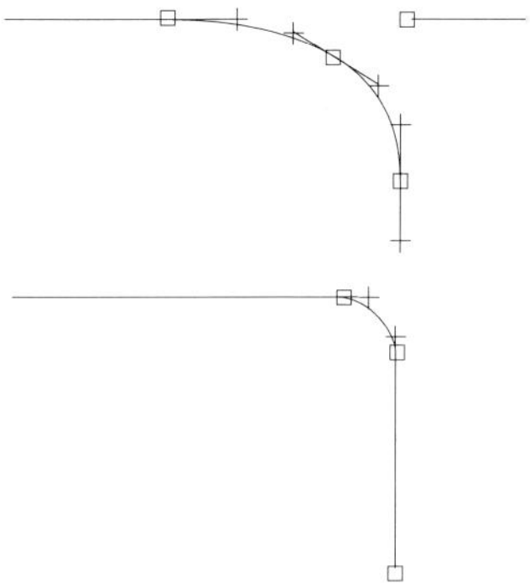

Figure 11. Transformation of line segments and deletion of paths.

Computer Compound Icons and their Families

Frutiger (1980, p.7) sees no division between the transformation from typographic form to symbol, one of his books on this subject entitled Type Sign Symbol 'draws a bridge from the printed character to the 'logotype or trademark and from there to the pictorial sign'. Going from type to symbol is very attractive to Frutiger, and the sign system and its typography for the Charles de Gaulle Airport between 1975 and 1976 demonstrate how the sign symbols work with the typography. Obviously letters work as a family and that symbols should also work as a family, and like type at different scales.[3] When greatly reduced

[3] Body text is normally between 8pt and 14pt, display type is anything above 14pt. Therefore character widths of strokes will be different depending on size. Symbols that are reduced require weight and width to be taken into consideration.

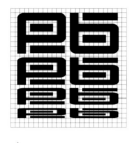

a)

b)

Figure 12. a) Symbol within a grid structure. b) Symbol, names and the emblem of Belize applied to stationary.

and reproduced on the Air France timetable (figure 13b, page 102). Modernist Constructivism from one medium to another have converged upon the Apple user interface. Like any evolutionary process the influence of high profile design such as Olympic games, and airports are as Ferdinand de Saussure suggests, synchronic, existing as state at a pivotal point (elite) in time, yet diachronic, having simultaneous (popular) appeal (Crystal, 1971, p.158). Frutiger (1980, p.42-43) considers that 'to discern the path of human discovery in the keystone of the past and at the same time in the foundation stone of the future'. Frutiger (ibid, p.98) then goes on to point out that 'from the mental store of pictures seen and signs learned, which we gather in our subconscious throughout our lives, shapes are called out, considered, compared with others, associated and superimposed, with one picture calling forth another'.

Frutiger's signs for Charles de Gaulle Airport are a family, but, for the computer icon what are really needed are compound icon elements that are interchangeable. In the same way as the corporate symbol has been developed, a family of computer icons can be used to inform through what they represent and to visually unify the interface. To evaluate the evolution of computer icon design standards it is important to understand the methods used to design families of symbols to see how interchangeability can work. Stuart Mealing explored the development of the pictographic symbols used in the Olympic events using four graphic representations from different dates (figure 14, page 102). The first image illustrating the Olympic wrestling event is drawn realistically, the last being the most graphically sophisticated. Each is designed to operate within a family group and each group reflects the graphic style of the period in which it was designed. It is the three later designs that reflect the grid architecture that allows for the transition from simplified pictures to a sophisticated abstraction. The 1964, 1968 and 1972 Olympic designs could have easily been designed with the interface clearly in mind, indeed Stuart Mealing (1991, p.63-69) draws his analogy of reproduction constraints from the pixel matrix for computer icons).

After Alan Kay and his team of engineers developed the principles of the SmallTalk interface at Xerox PARC, Apple graphic designers developed his ideas further for user interfaces (see Chapter 2 and 3). Kay and his team had determined how the interface was to interact with users leaving graphic designers with a fixed icon matrix, as Frutiger concludes they would have been subconsciously influenced by the design of symbols up to this point in time. Yoshiro Yamashita utilised the form of Isotype but not the essence of its syntax for the Tokyo Olympic games, and it does not go unnoticed the influence of modernism on Neurath. Ernst Gombrich CBE (1975, p.443) writes that during the first half of this century 'the future belonged to those who decided to begin afresh and to rid themselves of this preoccupation with style or ornament'. So at this point there is an opportunity for computer compound icons to develop using the essence of Isotype syntax, but also taking on the style of contempory symbol design for transport, Olympics and so on, adapting this to the medium of the interface and to the size of the pixel matrix. The design techniques have therefore been transported from drawing boards to computers through the methodology used in symbol design. Frutiger's style of drawing hands as symbols is not dissimilar to the the hand element that is used to represent an application program, complete with cuffs (figures 13a and 13b).

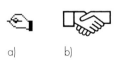

a)   b)

Figure 13. a) Computer icon element, and b) Frutiger's welcome symbol.

What is different between a corporate symbol, a family of symbols and more recently a family of computer icons is that they have to consider a multitude of permutations when being designed. The 1972 Munich Olympic symbols were designed using a horizontal, vertical and diagonal grid (figure 16). Allen Hulbert (1978, p.24) states that Otto Aicher's grid design for

1948

1964

1968

1972

Figure 14. Progression of Olympic symbols, 1948, 1964, 1968 and 1972 (reproduced from Dreyfuss).

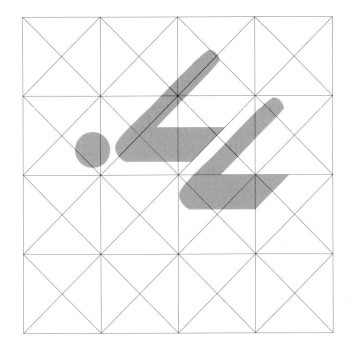

Figure 15. Aicher's horizontal, vertical and diagonal grid for the 1972 Munich Olympic Game.

Figure 15. Aicher took over the role of art director for the Munich Olympic Game and produced an interchangeable body alphabet that was simpler in design to the previous Tokyo Olympic Games symbols of Yoshiro Yamashita who according to Yukio Ota (1993, p.108) was inspired by Isotype.

the games also contained interchangeable elements that made up a 'body alphabet'. To design a symbol family requires the designer to consider every possible combination of uses for the elements. For computer icons this represents every possible action, but must also be flexible enough for future developments. To design a symbol as part of a visual family, with each symbol conveying a different message requires consideration of how every design element will work together. The design process has to be carried out across a broad front, and if one symbol within the family fails then adjustments will have to be made for part or all the family range (figure 15). Every computer operating system upgrade adds more functions, and like the Olympic symbols an opportunity to reflect upon contempory graphics without altering any established lexicon, but merely to exploit new possible capabilities of the displaying medium through evolution and not revolution.

All computer icons and their families that have been discussed so far all fit within a conventional 32 x 32, or 16 x 16 (half size icon) pixel matrix. However, the Internet has seen rapid growth in corporate companies building large Internet and intranet sites. British Steel insist that 'the "up-front" page should be dynamic and icon driven such that general and functional information can be instantly accessed' (1999). Large organisations have departments or groups that maintain their corporate appearance, and therefore our perception of that company. These same groups now appear to be developing their own computer compound icon lexicon in a style that reflects their corporate image. For example, Pfizer let all third party Internet developers know that 'intranet projects have tended to avoid close scrutiny in the past for a plethora of reasons, however as the scale and business sensitivity of intranet projects has grown so has the need to control risk' (Pfizer, 1998). From this document has come the Pfizer Web Standards and Guidelines with its own icons directory and notes on how they should be used. This document goes on to say that Pfizer icons are based on various style guides from the Internet, and especially W3C (World Wide Web Consortium). The Pfizer home icon represents the company headquarters and is based upon that building (figure 17).

The document does however, point towards the natural growth and change of icons and that Pfizer wish to encourage third party developers 'ideas and creativity'. The icons contained in the Icon Directory have instructions attached that also offer advice on the page location of the icon, which icons work best on dark backgrounds, which work best on light backgrounds and so on. Because many of the general icons have been taken from various style guides they are recognisable for what they are from other application programs such as the magnifying glass, folder, spanner and so on. The icons that are least recognisable are those that are specific to the business activities of Pfizer, such as the Research Administration Services link icon. The intended purpose of a directory and style guide for an intranet is so that each employee becomes familiar with

General Icons

Home

Help

Search

Up

Specific Icons

Discovery Research

Clinical

Research Administration

Figure 17. Pfizer icons from the Image Directory.

a)

b)

c)

d)

Figure 18. Representative navigation computer icons on the Proline website, South Korea.

the icons' intended use, and also expected location on the screen. However, many of their icons are larger than the 32 x 32 pixel matrix (figure 17).

James Cimino (1997, p.54) states that 'perhaps the most profound change will be brought about by corporate intranets will be social, not technological'. Many Pfizer icons represent precisly this, from the resturant menu, the local bus timetable through to the social and sports activities that are available. This also encourages groups that might not necessarily be aware that they share a common interest to be brough together through the intranet. Although many of the icons that Pfizer use are specific to that community, Internet interface icons share similar objectives through electronic commerce. Websites developed outside of Western culture might contain stilted English, but in the two examples of South Korean web development companies Proline and Nexon, the iconography used as navigation within these sites show little cultural difference in how the icons explain themselves. Indeed, Proline use representative icons which need little explanation. In the example below, the first icon represents a return to the homepage (figure 18a). The next icon clearly shows that it is a folded magazine (figure 18b), and the Youngsan Shopping icon indicates that the following pages contain computer equipment for sale (figure 18c). The final icon can be found on many Internet and intranet sites such as Pfizer, but also in the toolbox of many different application programs to represent taking a closer look (1998) (figure 18d).

Unlike Proline, Nexon use abstract icons which need further explanation. On rollover, the icons display what the action is; new, introduction, portfolio and so on. Nexon's use of abstract icons (figure 19, page 106) is no different from MediaLab Arts (UK) navigational icons for their CD (figure 20, page 107). Both interfaces have been designed along the same principles as to how they further explain what the icons mean, and both have a dependence on the use of letterform (figures 19 and 20). The staff of Proline and Nexon in Korea are Korean, yet both companies are owned and controlled from America. One assumption is that the entertainment icon was an abstract representation of rows of people in a cinema or theatre (see proximity, chapter 3). The designer, Dave Kennerly of Nexon (USA) makes clear that this is not so, the icon is an abstract form of the letter 'E' for entertainment (figure 19d). He also points out that the use of 'i' for information is commonly used in Korea, hence 'i' equals 'news' (figure 19a) (see also Chapters 2 and 6). Also, when asked about the difference between Nexon Korea and Nexon United States Kennerly adds that 'the corporate page www.nexon.co.kr [Korea] and www.nexon.net [USA] are nearly identical. Nexon Korea's homepage was imported with minimal changes'. This indicates that there is a general perception of developers that interfaces are universal.

Both websites use letterform which is an abstract representation of a sound value (see Chapter 1). The simpler and more graphically reduced an image element is, the easier it is to remember as a form, but first it has to be learned or it could be misinterpreted, like the example of the 'E' above (figure 19d). The MediaLab Arts interface icons, like Nexon need further explanation. Nexon's reason for this approach is that Nexon Korea are also the number one game provider to Internet Game Cafes (according to Kennerly, Game Cafes are nearly unheard of in the USA). Therefore, users learn the meaning of their game websites through return visits, 'all of this works because of their interrelationships with all Nexon game sites . . . two examples are the "parcel mail" and "n-mail" (nexus mail) icons. They both show arrows shooting across the screen to tell you that you have new mail. However, one indicates a game object, while the other a more "BBS" like article of mail.' This helps users to distinguish between n-mail which is specific to the game, and email that is graphically the same as most icons used to describe mail found in conventional email software. Consistent application of these icons help in the recognition of both, so that users can distinguish between the two.

There is nothing unusual in this approach, indeed if you consider a large multi-national company and its identity, similar analogies can be made. For example, the shop front of

a) New

b) Introduction

c) Portfolio

d) Entertain

e) Contact

f) Site Map

Figure 19. Graphically reduced abstract computer icons on the Nexon website, South Korea.

a) Information

b) Computing Information

c) Facilities

d) Introduction

e) Research

f) Students

Figure 20. Graphically reduced abstract computer icons on the MediaLab CD, United Kingdom.

McDonalds is common regardless of country. Sassoon and Gaur (1997, p.69) describe the illuminated McDonald's sign in Tianamen Square as having Chinese script added. The script does not remove the impact of the McDonald identity because it has sufficient space between it and the brand mark. On entry, all is familiar even in a country that is foreign to users. You might not be able to read the menu but you would recognise the food on offer (1998). A further analogy, and one that is probably closer to the two Korean examples above, would be the design of a BP petrol station where the exterior and interior conform to a corporate identity. Users are again familiar with how everything works and what should be done to get petrol. There are however subtle changes, such as the food sold in the shop which would be specific to the tastes of the country in which the petrol station is located (BP have 14,000 Petrol Stations in 26 countries) (1998).

Shinbiro (meaning a new and mystical road to the Internet) is a large Internet Service Provider owned by the Hyundai Information Technology Corporation. It felt it necessary to design a Korean interface as well as an interface for English speakers. Many of the navigational icons are the same for both but they have been presented in different ways, while other icons are different in each cultural version. Jin Young Choi (1998) is the webmaster for Shinbiro, and he points out that the English version is for the non-Korean who lives in Korea as the English version would be used differently, and would also inform users about life in Korea. But Shinbiro's real audience is the online Korean community, therefore the site has different scales and versions between English and Korean (figure 21, 22 and 23). Choi goes further and points out that he did consider the cultural differences for the design of both including the typography, but that the separate feel to each site was mainly determined by the different content. Choi describes the criteria used to decide which iconic metaphors were used:

Intuition is globally acknowledged by anyone!
Internet card service icon is envelop and card,
scheduler service s is personal diary book etc.
Internet service has been emerged by westerners,
spreads into all over the World, and people who
access the Internet breath in their internet
culture in easy way and at the almost same time.
So we koreans have similar intuition with them.
We still have some barriers such as ambiguity
between prior data communication service like
Compuserv and Internet online service, and how
to release the cultural shock and to reduce the
cultural abuse in technical and porno issues.

a)

b)

c)

d)

e)

Figure 22. Shinbiro interface icons for the Korean
version.

Figure 21. Shinbiro interface icons for the English version.

The icons above illustrate the different uses of the Shinbiro
website. However, it was pointed out that future upgrades of the
English version will contain the same features found in the
Korean version. Indeed the meaning of the Korean version can
be understood without reference to a translation, for example in
the Korean version of the icons above the first icon represents
internet shopping (figure 22a), and this element is used as a
part of the icon of the 'Weekly' banner to represent the same
activity (figure 21). The next icon represents an online paging

service, (figure 22b) while the next icon clearly shows a newspaper and goes directly to a choice of online news services such
as the *Korea Herald, Yonhap News, Digital Chojum* and so on
(figure 22c). The heart has been discussed earlier in this
chapter and has been combined with an envelope to represent
Internet greeting cards, (figure 22d) while the final icon represents an Internet roaming account, so that Shinbiro account
holders can make a local Internet connection from anywhere in
the world when travelling outside of Korea (figure 22e).

a)   b)   c)   e)   f)   g)

Figure 23. Shinbiro Korean only interface icons.

The mood of the Korean site is less serious in its presentation,
even though the style of the interface iconography is similar, a
clear distinction can be seen between the style of the Korean
script (figure 23) and the typography used on the English
version, (figure 21, left) as well as the choice of colour between
the English grey banner and the brightly coloured Korean background. The first icon represents downloading public domain
software (figure 23a), while the next icon contains a series of
hearts to denote the different specialist interest groups. Once
entered the heart has other elements infixed within the compound icon to denote what the interest group might possibly be
(figure 23b). The next two icons represent email, with its association with envelopes, (figure 23c) and playing computer
games through the 'joy stick' (figure 23e). The last two are not
so obvious, but when viewed in the context of what this site
actually is, then WebTV (figure 23f) and bookmarking your
place within the site become apparent. Users of the Shinbiro
website are expected to return, and like the icon design strategy
for the British Steel graduate recruitment website navigation to

information should be instantly accessible (see page 176, Tonga) through icon recognition which have been learned through previous visits. To achieve this it is important to know what factors impact upon user leaning and comprehension.

Figure 24. Smily emotion icons.

Both the Korean and English versions allow for email and chat-room conversations. To further aid understanding any messages sent can have an additional icon added to the message, to express the mood of the sender (figure 24b). This family series of 'smily face' icons are common, especially the first icon which has universal usage and can be found on a range of products other than computer interfaces (1998). Reuters use the icon throughout their website (1998). There is little difference between the Reuters 'smily face' (figure 24a) and the Korean (figure 24b), apart from the graphic style. Reuters use the icon to indicate 'oddly enough' stories across their website. The intended purpose of these daily updated stories from Reuters is to be 'uplifting' for users, they will be entering the web page expecting to receive precisely that. The mood of the story has been informed by the icon. David Armstrong, William Stokoe and Sherman Wilcox (1995, p.8) believe that 'what we write down is stripped of its emotional content and much of its communicative intent'. By adding gestural iconography the intent of the message has been communicated first.

Conclusion

To evaluate the evolution of computer compound icon design standards that enhance syntax it is important to understand the methods used to design a symbol and then a family of symbols to see how interchangeability can work. Designs that reflect the grid architecture allow each element to be considered for its own merit and the visual reading order in which it should appear. Therefore, symbols are normally made up of graphic elements brought together as one image that will have an overall connotation, which does not necessarily need to be understood, the symbol needs only to be recognised for what it denotes, not what it says. Computer compound icon syntax is different in that what the elements represent and the meaning that each has is important if they they denote is to be understood. Therefore whenever possible computer icons use real-world analogies to aid memorisation of computer syntax, that will normally be only one action. A symbol that is used to convey an overall concept of what an organisation is or does can be abstract, it is learned through consistent application and rigid guidelines as to how it is used. Each follows a different route in how they become associated with what they represent.

To design a symbol requires the designer to consider what the potential of the symbol's elements actually are and also what the point of departure is between typographic elements and symbols, as well as what optical considerations through scale affect both what has enabled computer icons to navigate through so many systems of symbol and visual syntax to take their present form and function. Achiers' body alphabet clearly demonstrates these points, so to design an icon as part of a family (see chapter 3, figures 9 and 13), with each icon conveying a different action requires consideration of how every design element will work together. Like Achiers' body alphabet the design process for computer compound icons has to be carried out across a broad front, and if one icon within the family fails then adjustments will have to be made for part or all the family range. For computer compound icons this represents every possible action, but must also be flexible enough for future developments that might be influenced by contempory design without disrupting any established syntax.

Kay's original interface design for SmallTalk, and how this concept was applied to the Apple interface might go unchallenged, but is this not such as bad thing as the development of language needs basic elements to form a lexicon. The aesthetic limitation of a matrix makes website icons that are greater than 32 x 32 pixels appear overly large when systems icons demonstrate that all the necessary information such as reading order can convey syntax. When icons are larger than the 32 x 32 pixel matrix they appear clumsy for what they are, because the standard has been set. Also, as at the time of inception subliminal images are formed from a mental store of visual pivotal moments, therefore with the size of the matrix and the single action function, compound icons then took on the style and form that has fundamentally remained since they were first introduced. By accepting something as a standard gives a consistency to computer icons and helps in their recognition. Elements that now appear on different websites from around the world help syntax through the formation of a lexicon. This indicates that a common culture which is shared through computer networks is forming, but knowing what further factors impact upon user learning and comprehension would help to identify which elements might work best when measured against syntactically similar elements.

Evaluating Representative and Abstract Computer Compound Icons

Previous chapters have explained that the design of computer compound icons from Apple through to Microsoft are regarded as a design 'benchmark', both in the size of the compound icon and also being representative of what they are. It is from these icons that a baseline for the natural selection of visual syntax forms. Core compound icon elements which survive and become reused tend to be those that are applicable to common verbs, such as email, search and so on, and these are also activities which are used across a wide range of computer programs and websites. The purpose of this chapter is to better understand what is accepted, by analysing user understanding between representative and abstract computer compound icons, and icons that are common to many interfaces and those that are specific to one interface that require a learning investment. These categories of compound icon can be measured at a level of meaningfulness through the same interface between an agreed lexicon and one where the denotative and connotative values are left to the test subjects to interpret. The implementation of this is through a transnational research project which is explained as a case study where dispersed work groups mediate through computers.

First, it is important to establish a method of measurement between abstract and representative notation, and whether what is being denoted can be further explained. Gerald Lohse *et al.* (1994, p.36-49) proposed rating on a scale from 1 to 10 with a choice of 10 categories, which are 'spatial - nonspatial, nontemporal - temporal, hard to understand - easy to understand, concrete - abstract, attractive - unattractive, emphasises whole - emphasises parts, nonnumeric - numeric, static structure - dynamic process, conveys a lot of information - conveys little information'. The Lohse model contains many categories for research into a range of visual classifications such as maps, cartograms, photo-realistic pictures and so on. Stuart Mealing and Masoud Yazdani (1990, p.133-136) state that 'it is practical to categorise icons (in the manner of Marshall Mchuhan) in terms of 'temperature' of information which they convey, according to their position on an axis stretching from pictures to symbols, and on their level of animation'(figure 1). Although other factors, as described by Lohse also apply to icons in varying degrees, it is Mealing and Yazdani that identify the main categories.

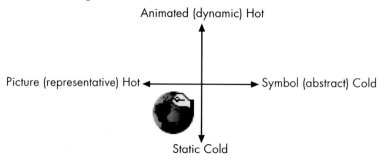

Animated (dynamic) Hot

Picture (representative) Hot ← → Symbol (abstract) Cold

Static Cold

Figure 1. Rating the comprehension of icons through the analogy of temperature. The icon shown illustrates its state on this page, as static and between concrete and abstract representation.

The compound icon illustrated is neither a picture of the world, nor an abstract symbol of what it denotes. Also the compound icon has a second element added, which has taken on meaning to denote an application. The denotation of the compound icon represents building (program) the World Wide Web. Further meaning through 'acting out' (animating) the actions, would help to confirm meaning. There is also the diagram itself. Unlike the icon element that represents the Earth the arrows illustrating the compound icons position within a diagrammatic scale are not natural, they do not represent direction. One culture, the Maya, understood direction through colour, which is no different from an arrow taking on meaning as direction, although it could be argued that it implies direction through – spear, arrow and therefore direction (figure 2a). Yukio Ota (1993, p.58) states that in the North American Indian writing system 'one arrow on top facing right and another arrow below facing left mean war'. However, arrows are a fundamental graphic element because they are consistently used in certain communities in a directional context. Of this Harm Zwaga and Ronald Easterby (1978, p.287) conclude that 'the arrow has some potency in conveying the intended meaning'. The results of a comprehension test by them for the ISO symbol that denotes 'escalator-up' demonstrated that most respondants understood that it was an esculator, yet none could tells its direction until an arrow was added.

The ABC's of Graphic Symbols

It should not be readily assumed that what something represents will be common to all, it has been learned and depends upon the rules of that community. Traffic signs are made-up of family groups which contain what Henry Dreyfuss (1972, p.26) describes as a 'basic to semiotic communication . . . They are the foundation – the ABC's – of graphic symbols'. In this respect, as a fundamental element they are no different to arrows, except that arrows normally supplement meaning rather than imply context which basic shapes provide. The traffic sign warning triangle, like the circle used for permission and restriction has other elements added to it to denote what the warning actually is. As a foundation graphic element, nearly all respondents to the questionnaire identified the triangle correctly (see Chapter 2, page 42) (figure 2b). Phil Barnard and Tony Marcel (1978, p.43) during a NATO conference on visual presentation of information state that 'as with language, their effective use nevertheless relies heavily on assumptions concerning learning, pre-existing knowledge and situational context'. Of this Dreyfuss (1972, p.142) wrote that 'a drawing of the skull and crossbones was displayed to a group of three-year-olds. "PIRATES" they screamed. But when I drew the outline of a bottle around the symbol, they immediately shouted "POISON"'. The arrow might imply direction, infixed within a restriction circle and used in the correct context denotes that it is a direction that is forbidden.

Symbols used as part of corporate identity give an overall representation of what that company is/does through the choice of elements that make-up the symbol. As explained previously (see Chapter 4), great effort is required to associate the organisation with the symbol – learning the association is through rigorous application. However, this does not require the viewer to understand what the elements within the design of the symbol actually denote. What Casper Werkman (1974, p.91) says of this is that 'even an incorrect interpretation of a device-mark may not prevent the mark from performing its function'. For example, students from the Faculty of Arts at the University of Plymouth were asked to identify the University logo, all recognised the symbol for what it denotes without hesitation. When these same students were then asked to describe their understanding of the University's identity, none saw the connotation of the South West Peninsula within (figure 3a). Of this Wally Olins (1982, p.82) writes that 'the reputation of Shell is symbolised to a quite extraordinary extent by its name and visual imagery. If there were no single name, no symbol, no colours, there would be no single, simple idea of Shell'.

The Apple logo was designed by Regis McKenna in 1977. Olins (ibid, p.69) cites the marketing men after having brainstorming sessions about Apple's identity as having 'wrung their hands and ended up with a weak compromise. "Call the company after a fruit and sell the product like a transistor radio? You must be crazy"'. If a connotation is not necessarily there an object that already has implied meaning will attach to that connotation. John Foley (1993, p.187) cites Jean-Louis Gassee, a former Vice-President of Apple Computers as having said 'one of the deepest mysteries to me is our logo – the symbol of lust and knowledge, bitten into, all crossed with colours of the rainbow in wrong order. You couldn't dream of a more appropriate logo: lust, knowledge, hope and anarchy' (figure

a)

b)

Figure 2. Arrows, triangles and so on are fundamental symbols, but they do not naturally denote what they mean which is also true of the '!', they have been learned according to the rules of a community.

3b). Abstract symbols that have real-world counterparts and clearly represent what they are can also elude interpretation. Foley (ibid, p.175) writes that in 'September 1990, to symbolise their party as "alive, soaring and free-spirited", British Liberal Democrats adopted a gold "bird of liberty" (their previous, diamond-shaped logo resembled the "baby on board" symbol on car rear windows)' (figure 3c).

a)   b)   c)

Figure 3. a) When a group of students were shown the University logo all recognised the symbol, yet none recognised the South West of England Peninsula. b) The Liberal Democrat logo is easier to recognise what the connotation is, both are abstract symbols.

Charles Bliss developed a simple system of one hundred basic symbols that could be combined in any combination to express a fundamental meaning in any language. Bliss applied this to specific applications within science, industry, commerce, traffic and so on. Bliss (Dreyfuss, 1972, p.22) described Semantography as 'a simple system of pictorial symbols which could be read (like 1 + 2 = 3) in all languages – without translation. It would also contain a simple symbolic logic and semantics . . . It operates with about 100 basic symbols which can be combined for any meaning needed in communication'. The Bliss directional equivalent contains a dot placed above or below a line. The dot denotes that the object of the subject is above or below, or if the size of the dot is increased as in sunrise or sunset, meaning directional, as the sunsets in the west, and the sunrise rises in the east (but not in the sense of Maya syntax, see Chapter 1). Dot and line have been reduced to the 'coldest' connotation, context and a learned lexicon explain meaning, without this it is simply a dot and a line (Bliss, 1965, p.117) (figure 4a). However, there are other Bliss symbols that are self-explaining, such as an envelope that can have other elements in association to denote the type of envelope, (figure 4b) this is not disimilar to Isotype in how they work (ibid, p.137) (figure 4c).

a) below, above   b) Envelope + to fly = airmail c) plane + envelope = airmail

Figure 4. a) and b) Blissymbolics (reproduced from Bliss), and c) Isotype (reproduced from Neurath)

The Elephants Memory is a computer visual language not dissimilar to Blissymbolics which allows the user to construct a visual message by combining symbols from a vocabulary of approximately 150 separate graphic elements. These elements have a syntactic order of arrangement within the system as an essential part of its visual grammar. Timothy Ingen-Housz (1996) developed the system as 'a metaphor of language learning'. The software consists of a series of 'dragable sprites' which triggers a response when the elements are combined into a message. This interactivity allows the user of the program to build a visual sentence. However, because of the limited vocabulary many elements change meaning according to the context in which they are used. This is opposite to the Maya writing which has many visual elements that have the same meaning (see Chapter 1, page 32). With Ingen-Housz because the lexicon is limited core elements such as the 'x' can mean start, stop, nothing, death and so on (figures 5b and 5d), while the flash from the gun can mean shout instead of shoot, if the element is joined with the mouth (figure 5).[1] When elements have multiple meaning the whole message needs to to viewed if the elements that make-up the message are to be understood. Masoud Yazdani and Dorian Goring (1990, p.3) observed that like Blissymbolics and the Elephants Memory the pictographic writing of the North American Indian was also, 'elemental, basic, logical and largely idiomatic', and like Bliss and Ingen-Housz was also to be viewed first to ensure the context of the message was understood before being read.

[1] Viewable at www.khm.de/~timo

Actor, object/event, associative field   The whole city   None of the birds

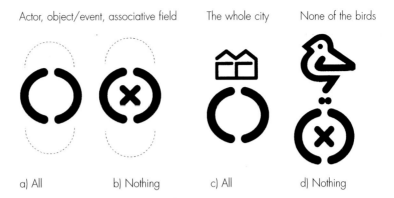

a) All   b) Nothing   c) All   d) Nothing

Figure 5. An example of the Elephants Memory grammar.

Figure 6. Ingen-Housz's visual language if viewed from left to right would read, 'I saw on the television, many (plural infliction, associative field) young men shooting elephants (plural infliction, associative field)'.

As in the development of many other visual language systems the Elephants Memory groups units of meaning together for example, 'I hear the rabbit' (figure 7a), 'I hear several rabbits' (figure 7b). The graphic elements are clear, the rabbit, arrow and ear are free from ambiguity. The associated fields and their position allow for further denotation, the two dots below the rabbit (figure 7b, see also figure 6 above, young men and elephants, plural association) inform us that there are many rabbits (plural, associative field), and the 'actor' representation of 'self,' above the ear in both illustrations informs the receiver who is hearing (associative field). We know that the event is to hear the rabbit, and not to listen for rabbits because of the direction of the arrow (origin/way/media/destination indicator). Other elements can be added, the telephone (figure 7c), now alters the message to, 'I hear the rabbit on the telephone'. By changing the direction of the arrow, the message now means that, 'I am listening to several rabbits on the telephone' (figure 7d). This is a major semantic change, but a subtle distinction between the graphic elements.

Adrian Frutiger (1991, p.120) observes that the Sumerian writing was 'limited to the essentials'. His assumption is that this was probably due to the fact that the pictographs were scratched on the outside of containers as a record of trade (figure 8a, 8b, 8c, 8e and 8d). Pictographic similarities can be easily identified in the Elephants Memory, with the early Sumerian sign for man (penis) and woman (vulva) which are only separated by the medium of their display and the tools that created them (figures 8e and 8f).[2] The pictographs used by the early Sumerians would have been chosen for utility to represent what they are. The elements used for Ingen-Housz's system are also identifiable for what they are, it is the grammar for how they are used which has to be learned (figure 8f).

a) I hear the rabbit.

b) I hear several rabbits.

c) I hear the rabbit on the telephone.

d) I am listening to several rabbits on the telephone.

Figure 7. Objects, actor, direction, plural infliction within three association fields.

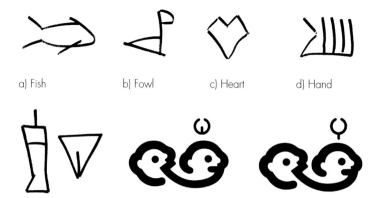

a) Fish   b) Fowl   c) Heart   d) Hand

e) Male and female   f) Someone speaks to the woman, someone speaks to the man. Additions can be made to the associative field to name the speaker and so on.

Figure 8. Similarities can be seen between pre-cuneiform Sumerian.

Figure 9. Exchange and Trade. The two 'actors' are taking something from each other.

[2] Early Sumerian pictograms underwent radical change 5,000 years ago, and is probably due to changing from scratching to impressing a stylus into clay which creates wedge shapes known as cuneiform.

History informs us that human transactions have always needed to record and convey information – this fundamental requirement has changed little since the first Sumerian commercial transactions were scratched on the outside of containers some 6,000 years ago. Likewise the Elephants Memory demonstrates these principles through the notion of object/value and trade (figure 9). These object/value elements are joined to the 'actors' to denote that a transaction is taking place. Again these grouped elements can have other object/value elements assigned to alter the meaning. The Mixtec and Aztec both spoke different languages, so they found it unnecessary to evolve beyond pictographic and ideographic signs. Both cultures could communicate and trade through the script. David Kelly (1976, p.166) is a Mesoamerican scholar and linguist, and believes that the primitive nature of ideographic scripts used by the Mixtec and Aztec scribes was 'one of the crowning achievements of Mesoamerican culture, which might well be adopted, with appropriate modifications, for international commerce today'.

Investment in learning a system needs purpose, and Ingen-Housz recognises that 'as the internet turns into a global multilingual community, the project searches for new ways to bridge cultures, and to build transitional spaces between natural languages'. Trade was one of the concerns of Bliss developing his system. If Ingen-Housz's semantic environment is to work then incentives such as trade must be central to the Elephants Memory and be of a greater advantage than present communication modes either spoken, written or iconic. Blissymbolics had many hopes, but was never adopted for the same reasons. For a system that requires learner investment it must have incentives. Complexity of grammar within the Elephants Memory goes beyond the requirements of a utilitarian language. Sumerian writing was developed through trade, it was not an additional writing system, which was also true of Mixtec and Aztec ideographs. Computer compound icons demand little learning from users if they have been borrowed from other systems or where the same compound icons has been consistently reapplied, as unnatural and forced developments of a system tends to be regulated by the needs of users.

The Trotman Publishing group produce a range of graduate recruitment publications in print and as websites for a range of large corporate organisations. Within the Trotman website is a messaging centre which is only accessible by Trotman clients.[3] The message centre uses modes of communication that are written or iconic where appropriate, never forcing users to overly invest in time learning a lexicon or indeed a whole new system such as Blissymbolics or the Elephants Memory. It should also be recognised that users have independently devised a fixed emoticon lexicon (mixture of letters, parenthesis and so on). Emoticons attempt to imply the tone of the message by trying to substitute a visual equivalent of the nuances of typography that can give a message added meaning according to the choice of typeface, size and weight, whereas email can only express itself through the interplay of upper and lower case within a fixed size and font. Indeed, to use uppercase is considered as 'shouting' at the message receiver. Through being confined to the keyboard

[3] The centre contains link buttons to the original brief, contact details, work progress and schedule. A further dialogue box on the screen allows users to scroll through previous message headings. There is also a series of link buttons within the client and Trotman dialog box which are specific to that client.

Figure 10. Trotman online messaging centre first prototype, the second prototype has less depth, network speed of delivery is balanced against aesthetics. The face ideographs are adopted from Shinbiro (see Chapter 4, page 110).

[4] Emoticons are a natural progression of language, developed by the users and not by a designed system.

emoticons have become standardised and used within email to convey the emotion of the message sender – :-) Basic happy – :-(Basic sad. Simpler emoticons are easily learned and regularly used, while other more complex emoticons require a learning investment for both encoder and decoder {:V (duck), (_8(|) (Homer Simpson). This combination of expression is confined to the lexicon available from the keyboard, where there are approximately 120 emoticon combinations which can be com- bined with a phonetic alphabet.[4]

Recognising this apparent fundamental need to give a message further meaning the Trotman messaging centre uses a family of compound icons as suggested in Chapter 4 by David Armstrong, William Stokoe and Sherman Wilcox, (1995, p.8) when writing in the messages dialog text cannot easily imply the intent and mood of the message, so the emoticons lexicon still needs to be learned. Therefore the message dialog contains six faces which are faded into the background, but become fully visible when selected. These faces are ideographs of what the facial expression implies, apart from 'happy' and 'sad' the meaning, of the other four are 'laugh', 'I'm unsure', 'surprise' and 'the side ways glance – what do you mean'. The lexicon although self-explaining has a help facility which enables indi- vidual captions when the 'pointer' activates the icons, also in the previous messages dialog the subject heading is augmented with the appropriate face as a memory prompt of what that message contains (figure 10).

However, interfaces now allow users at any geographical location to communicate words, sounds and images normally through a shared iconic computer interface. With international barriers reduced through the Internet, users are only separated by the differences of culture that are outside of computer interfaces. To users of computer interfaces the difference may only be noticeable by the language associated with a compound computer icon. It is the icon which provides the linkage to cross language barriers within the culture of shared user interfaces. This has facilitated the potential for change in how users work and how communication takes place across the Internet. Stephen Scrivener and Susan Vernon (1995, p.107-112) consider that:

> Design is often a collaborative or collective activity in which individuals with different skills and expertise work towards a shared goal. Furthermore, design is increasingly an activity with a global dimension; products are being designed for international markets. A future can be envisaged in which designers work as part of international teams supported by computer – and electronically-mediated communication.

At present computers are improving communications globally and the ways in which people communicate are undergoing great changes. The development of communication systems enables the transport of data quickly and reliably. Although most of the telecommunications infrastructure was chiefly constructed to support real-time verbal communications, the network is becoming a sophisticated means of communicating digital files created in a variety of media. Paul Wilson (1991, p.26) makes clear that gradual change to all-digital information formats is breaking down the barriers that have naturally developed in various disciplines and infrastructures. In turn this facilitates 'shared workspace, shared information and group activity support'. Ronald Easterby (1978, p.19) considers that 'as designers and evaluators of displayed information we are primarily concerned with the communication of messages, indeed this occurs at the intersection of the disciplines of psychology and graphic communication'. What Easterby concludes is that this already happens, if you consider corporate identity schemes designed for organisations 'the answer must at be at once psychological, graphical and technological'. If human-computer or human-computer-human communication is to be supplemented with compound icons then there should be an effective method of evaluation.

Aaron Marcus (1999) declares that 'shockingly, in some of our projects, our clients never do call in users . . . however, we work as designers to prepare prototypes that are then evaluated by users'. Judith Olson and Thomas Moran (1996, p.271-272) believe that for the evaluation of interfaces there are 'few complete methods'. They do however, consider that approaches such as 'Cognitive Walkthrough' allow designers to improve interfaces when users 'first walks up to it'. Cognitive Walkthrough asks questions of users about how easy it was for them to 'discover how to do the next step'. Olson and Moran go on to say that users should also be observed and invited to join and influence the design process. One problem is that the users then become removed from 'steping up' to the interface for the first time. They begin to form certain biases and assumptions that are no different from the designers themselves. A method for evaluating interfaces requires achieving results that are repeatable and possibly carried out on a test group or groups that have some incentive to engage with an interface. Before users 'step up' as Olson and Moran have already said they should first know what those benefits actually are and 'perhaps even enjoy using it'.

The ARC Interface

If learner investment is through incentive, to gain from that investment knowing what that investment is helps to decide how far a lexicon can go for a group that has an interest in using a particular interface. The ARC (Arts Research into Communication) was a series of innovative projects through 'virtual collaboration' with two institutions in the United

Kingdom, and one each from France and Spain, and between campuses of the University of Plymouth. This series of projects is known as the Atlantis InterArc EC Research Programme. The first phase established parity for shared screen and simultaneous voice communication via ISDN Planet II. The establishment of a 'Virtual Studio' at each location allowed each group to exchange files, see other computer screens at remote locations, and operate other computer systems. The purpose of the project was to evaluate the convergence of technology between computers and communication and the natural development of computer compound icons within the group. Comprehension of specific navigational interface icons were designed in such a way that the interface could track, monitor and report back user comprehension, learning time and navigational preferences.

Stuart Card, Thomas Moran and Allen Newell (1983, p.404) state that 'the basic performance variables of a human-computer system are concerned with what tasks the system can do (functionality), how long it takes to acquire the functionality (learning), how long it takes to accomplish tasks (time), how frequently errors occur and how consequential they are, how well tasks are done (quality)'. For this reason the title screen of the ARC has four hidden 'rollover' navigation points, all are visible on mouse-up, each individual compound icon is visible on rollover (since Java script has become widely used in the design of web pages, dynamic icon behaviour has become more common). Once these points are learned they continue to be located in the same positions in the actual content of the ARC and therefore, users learn the rollover positions and knows their navigational significance. The advantage of this is that the content is not cluttered with compound icons, leaving the graphical user interface clear to perform the functions of the ARC's content. The home screen contains all the navigational icon points, and on mouse-up users are required to return to the home screen via the initial set of rollover icons. The four hidden rollover icons on both the title and home screen remain constant throughout the CD. Once their position and action has been learned users can always expect to find them at these navigational points. These four compound icons represent the 'Oops button' which takes the user back one screen; 'Volume button' which adjusts the sound levels; 'Home screen button' which returns the user to the home screen; and 'Help button' which explains how to navigate, this is for users who are lost but would still like to browse the ARC (figure 11b).

a)   b)

Figure 11. a) The title screen for the ARC. b) On mouse-up all screen navigational icons are visible.

The home screen contains three of these icons, as the home screen button is not required. This screen contains a further two sets of compound icon. The first set is concerned with the classification of the contents of the ARC ie: Timebased, Sound, Still, and Interactive. These icons closely resemble each other, and because the differences are minimal their function is only apparent on mouse up when they become motion dynamic. These icons require users to make distinctions between icons which closely resemble each other. The only other distinguishing feature of the compound icon is their location. However, to track and monitor user learning, the icons are clustered closely together near the centre and bottom of the screen (figure 12b). Upon entrance to the content of the journal a second set of compound icons appear as a new bottom row. These additional icons are also designed as part of the representational family group of compound icons (figure 13b page 129, bottom row, beginning left).

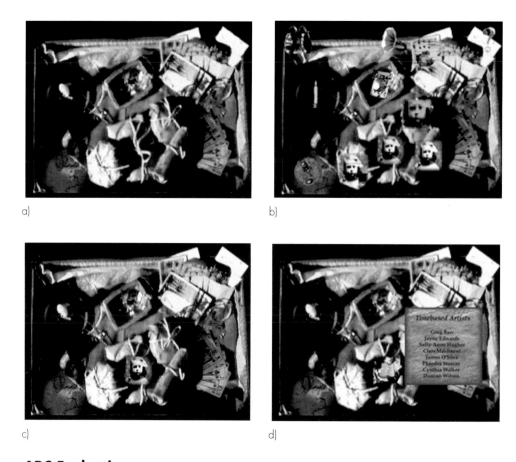

a)

b)

c)

d)

ARC Evaluation

To evaluate the ARC interface ten test subjects were asked to repeat the same task five times, the purpose of the task was to understand how users acquire the denotative values of interface metaphors. The test subjects were divided into two groups of five, and choice of group was left to individual members. Those who felt less confident about using a computer gravitated towards the 'with lexicon group' (Group A), wheras more experienced subjects saw a non-lexicon test as a challenge (Group B). After the grouping was decided each test subject was individually instructed, before launching the program. On entry to the program Group A were directed to the 'help' button, while Group B were told not to select help if

Figure 12 a) On entry no icons are visible.
b) Positions of all navigational icons. c) Timebased icon up on rollover. d) Animation of icon and selection window on mouse-up.

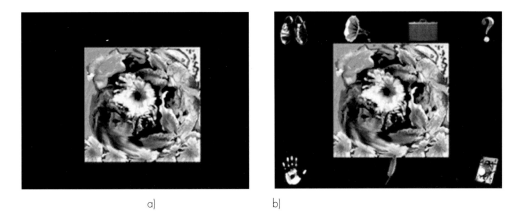

a)   b)

Figure 13. On entry no icons are visible. b) Positions of all navigational icons. Firstly listing the artists in that category, secondly comments by the originator of that specific work and, thirdly other titles of work by that artist contained within the ARC.

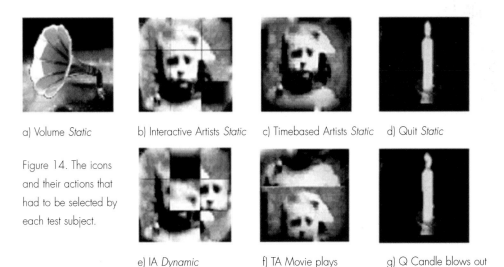

a) Volume *Static*

Figure 14. The icons and their actions that had to be selected by each test subject.

b) Interactive Artists *Static*   c) Timebased Artists *Static*   d) Quit *Static*

e) IA *Dynamic*   f) TA Movie plays   g) Q Candle blows out

that target compound icon was rolled over. The task for both groups was to locate and select (click) four navigational compound icons, and two dynamic compound icons that represented their function on selection; IA Interactive Artists (figures 14b static, 14e dynamic) and TA Timebased Artists (figure 14c static, 14f dynamic) – one static/representative; V Volume (figure 14a) – one dynamic/representative; Q Quit (figures 14dstatic, 14g dynamic). The task also had to be carried out in sequence, IA* TA* V* Q* (three attempts) and then change sequence to evaluate spatial memory to IA* TA* V* Q* (two attempts). This would generate five reports on each test subject.

The reports that were generated log the time spent at a target location. For example, 'starting now 1:51:26 pm Monday 22 February 1999, home screen at: 1:51:28 pm Monday 22 February 1999, rolled over volume at: 1:51:29 pm Monday 22 February 1999, changed volume at: 1:51:29 pm Monday 22 February 1999, home screen at: 1:51:31 pm Monday 22 February 1999'. This five second example shows that this user launched the program at 1:51:26, the cursor then moved across a non-target area (the home screen) until the volume control icon was reached three seconds later. The volume was changed immediately, the test subject then stayed within the volume control for a total of two seconds before moving on. The detail of the reports for 10 users record the average time spent on all five tasks as 4 minutes and 52 seconds generating 19,915 icon names, times, events and subsequent actions. A second report was written to extract the required data for each of the five attempts – duration, quit, time spent at the interface, return visits to icons, target icons that were rolled over, target icons that were selected (clicked), non-target icons that were rolled over or selected, and if the final sequence was accurate. The actual sequence was also included with selection indicated by *, and hit icon targets indicted with bold type. For example, 2D* TA 2D AN AN IA LG* Q* (figure 15, legend). The second report also allows for additional observations such as recovery time by the subject when off target. There are many occurrences in the later reports where the earlier reports indicate that the target icons have been visited, for example, in subject eight, the third report includes the recovery time between Q Q* as 1 second and between TA TA IA* as 2 seconds. These observations establish that the test subject understands the lexicon, but that the sequence was technically incorrect.

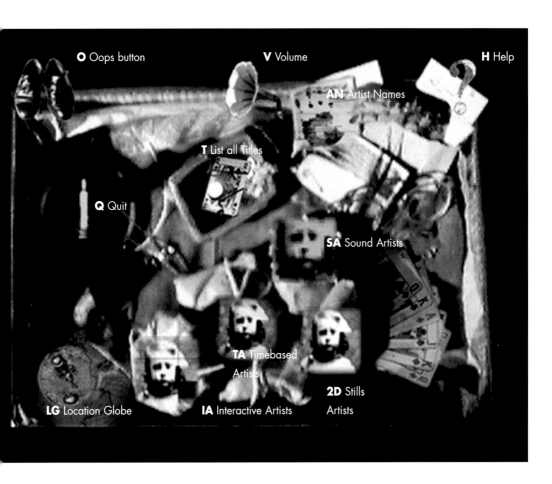

O Oops button   V Volume   H Help
AN Artist Names
T List all Titles
Q Quit
SA Sound Artists
TA Timebased Artists
2D Stills Artists
LG Location Globe   IA Interactive Artists

Within the data collection * indicates that a selection (click) by the user has been made.

Figure 15. Legend of all possible target icons. For example, actual sequence of test subject ten (Group B, without lexicon), first report O O AN H AN T Q LG IA IA TA 2D 2D LG* IA IA* TA TA* TA 2D T Q O V H V V TA V* O H H 2D TA T LG LG O H AN T Q LG IA TA 2D T Q T Q T Q T * Q* and test subject ten final report V* IA* TA* Q*.

The second report was used to generate a table of key interface events for all five reports, and included; technically incorrect, but where the subsequent reports show the sum total of correct target icon hits with no attempt to select the off target icon, and that the recovery time is within 3 seconds. On the second launch of the program four members of Group A had successfully

Returned Data from the Report Logs

Time Spent at Interface and Use of Lexicon

Minutes : seconds	**A** With Lexicon 5 Subjects					**B** Without Lexicon 5 Subjects				
	Time	1	2	3	4	Time	1	2	3	4
First Report	3:29	**0**	0	4	92	2:38	**0**	0	3	159
Second Report	0:26	**4**	2	5	7	1:23	**1**	0	3	91
Third Report	0:18	**5**	3	5	3	0:21	**4**	1	5	8
Changed Sequence										
Fourth Report	0:20	**5**	1	5	8	0:21	**4**	1	5	13
Fifth Report	0:13	**5**	3	5	2	0:15	**5**	2	5	4
Total Time Spent	4:46	Average at help 1:45				4:58				

Use of lexicon cont.	**A** With Lexicon 5 Subjects					**B** Without Lexicon 5 Subjects				
	5	6	7	8	9	5	6	7	8	9
First Report	74	68	**19**	6	142	90	133	**15**	12	150
Second Report	23	9	**20**	0	32	67	67	**16**	9	134
Third Report	23	1	**20**	0	24	28	4	**19**	0	32
Changed Sequence										
Fourth Report	29	2	**20**	0	31	33	4	**19**	0	37
Fifth Report	21	0	**20**	0	21	23	1	**20**	0	24

Figure 16. The Key data from these tables have been highlighted to show when full use of the lexicon is understood, and what those implications are across a range of interface events.

1. Technically Incorrect, but with lexicon understood (previous reports form each test subject show the sum total of correct icon target hits).
2. Technically correct with no OFF target hits and where all icons have been selected (clicked).
3. Number of subjects that have identified dynamic, static/representational and dynamic/representational target icons.
4. Return visits to OFF and ON target icons.
5. ON Target icons hit.
6. OFF Target icons hit.
7. Selected motion dynamic, static/representational and dynamic/representational ON target (excluding duplicate hits). 20 individual hits required for full lexicon.
8. Selected motion dynamic, static/dynamic representational OFF target (excluding duplicate hits).
9. Total icon hits.

selected all target icons, by the third attempt all members had been successful (figure 16.1). Group B fared less well and had not identified all target icons until the last attempt. During the first attempt all members of Group A, except one, had selected the target icons, whereas Group B members had not identified all target icons until the fifth attempt (figure 16.7). Learning time was greater during the first attempt by Group A with an average of 1 minute 45 seconds learning the lexicon and an average of 1 minute 44 seconds hunting for compound icon locations within the interface. Upon the second attempt, this group spent an average of 26 seconds attempting to accomplish the task. Group B took five times longer during the second attempt, and parity was reached during the third and subsequent attempts.

Group B hit nearly double the amount of target icons during their first attempt and 13 times more target icons during the second attempt (figure 16.4). This is partly due to a missing lexicon which was still incomplete for one member until the final attempt (figure 16.3). Also during the second attempt Group A returned to the target icons 12 more times than was necessary, whereas Group B returned 114 times to confirm the compound icons meaning (figure 16.9). Not all of these returns were to target icons, off target icons had to be explored so that they could be dismissed.

Low hits and no selection of the representational buttons are probably due to an attribute of the cursor that was not disclosed to either groups which was the 'all icons displayed' feature. This shows all interface icons when the mouse is held down on the home screen. All subjects found and used this feature from the first report to the last, and therefore all subjects were aware of representational compound icons on the interface. Non-target representational icons were hit such as 'Oops back one screen' but only three times by Group A and 22 times by Group B. Compared to other off target compound icons which need further explanation (T AN SA 2D and LG) the hit rate was low, and no test subject attempted to select the 'Oops' icon indicating that it did not represent a target compound icon.

Conclusion

Common compound icons have developed through natural selection, they are unambiguous with clear intention, but even these representative compound icons do not necessarily require their correct connotation to be understood, simply what they denote. This is similar to icons that require learning where the understanding of the compound icons connotation does not prevent its function from being understood. But users need purpose to learn specific icons and if there is no incentive then potentially users might simply give up. For example the group without lexicon stayed at the interface for 2 minutes and 38 seconds on their first attempt, and 1 minute 23 seconds on their second attempt. This appears to be a short time for a test subject to stay at the interface. Also, the amount of return visits on and off target are high and suggest that if this group did not have purpose then they would have probably given up. Blissymbolics had many hopes, but was never used. Ingen-Housz's semantic environment also requires incentives that appear disproportionate to potential gain. Through observation, if the ARC interface is compared with how users browse the Internet, it is noticeable that user attempt times to understand the navigation of a website appear even shorter, leaving the site if gain is minimal and can be found elsewhere. This also explains why there was only one return from the CADE CD which contained this version of the ARC. Other parts of the CD were simply easier to navigate. Computer compound icons that navigate should represent what they mean, and give a further explanation to confirm their meaning when selected, through a dynamic behaviour. By deploying user tracking compound icons can be evaluated, and those that are least successful can be exchanged allowing the interface to be re-evaluated through the data that is impartial and without bias.

It must be recognised as stated by Card, Moran and Newell (1983, p.404) that 'users vary widely in general intellectual ability, experience with computers, specific knowledge of the task, specific knowledge of the computer, cognitive style, and perceptual-motor skills . . . finally there are variables concerning the user's subjective feeling about the system'.

Navigating Interfaces

Chapter 5 identified that in order to learn a system of navigation through an iconic interface there must be incentives, and the icons that are used for navigation must be unambiguous with clear intention. Further tests are carried out to gauge user comprehension and assumption when using icons as navigation. This chapter then moves away from core graphic system icons which are normally pixel perfect and within a 32 x 32 matrix, to web page icons that vary in size according to the overall design of the website, and to explain how users navigate through websites. Comparisons are made between signing systems in public places, an Internet community and World Wide Web browser such as eWorld that uses an equivalent real-world metaphor throughout the interface with place, function and content icons. A publication that has a design standard that is comparable to the best of that sold in high street newsagents such as *MacUser* will be investigated to understand why design change is gradual and not dramatic, how readers navigate and what the long term implication is for established websites.

User Goals and Sub-goals

David Canter (1978, p.261) writes that 'to evaluate systems for people who have particular goals to achieve it is necessary to identify what those characteristics are which lead to people needing to rely upon the system provided. It is then necessary to identify what are the family of goals and sub-goals which these users are likely to have'. Stuart Card, Thomas Moran and Allen Newell (1983, p.10) write of applied psychology in the context of user goals and state that 'humans behave in a goal-

orientated way. Within their limited perceptual and informa-
tion-processing abilities, they attempt to adapt to the task environment to attain their goals'. Microsoft Word is one of many
word processing programs which enable users to carry out a
number of tasks – users have incentive to learn how to use this
program, but has to learn the lexicon to engage in a dialogue.
However, much of this can be achieved through a user's 'one-
way pidgin' version of human-computer discourse through
what they already know.[1] In order to address this Judith Olson
and Thomas Moran (1996, p.272) suggest that users must perceive a benefit from using the interface as it was intended.
However, many actions are learned and habits are formed
before this point is actually reached.

   Word is similar to other programs as to how it functions by
relying upon Apples original approach of 'hey you – do this'. As
pointed out in Chapter 2, to aid user comprehension requires
standardisation across programs. The program uses many icon
elements to build compound icons which are used within other
programs, yet it also uses icon elements that are specific to
Word. In order to gauge user comprehension 20 test subjects
were asked to use the program. This ensured that 'pointing and
clicking' on an icon was in context. The results were divided
into two groups, those that used Word as their main word processing program (14), and those that used a different word processing program (5, with 2 invalidated). All test subjects where
first year undergraduates who had recieved computer induction
before the test, all had used word processing programs, but not
necessarily Word (figure 1).

   Overall both groups paralleled each other in their comprehension of what individual and family groups of compound
icons meant. Although Denis McQuail and Sven Windahl
(1986, p.60) were discussing the effects of mass communication on culture and society, that relates mainly to 'influence
which is long term, unplanned, indirect and collective . . . our
attention is directed not as separate "messages", but at whole
sets or systems of messages which have similar features', they
were referring to informal learning of social roles and from

[1] In the sense that it is derived from a language, creates it's own method of use by adapting syntax and where the outcome is recognisable, but the method is not necessarily desirable.

Family Groups

	1	2	3	4	5	6	6	8	9	10	11	12
1) **User** Correct	12	12	10	14	11	10	5	2	12	1	-	5
2) Correct Context	1	-	1	-	1	-	-	2	-	4	5	6
3) Attempted/Incorrect	1	2	3	-	2	2	6	8	-	5	6	2
4) No attempt	-	-	-	-	-	2	3	2	2	4	3	1
5) **Non User** Correct	3	3	3	5	5	3	2	1	3	-	-	3
6) Correct Context	1	1	-	-	-	-	-	-	-	3	3	-
7) Attempted/Incorrect	1	-	2	-	-	2	2	4	1	-	-	-
8) No Attempt	-	1	-	-	-	-	1	-	1	2	2	2

	13	14	15	16	17	18	19	20	21	22
1) **User** Correct	11	6	5	8	8	1	4	4	-	7
2) Correct Context	-	1	4	2	2	7	1	2	1	-
3) Attempted/Incorrect	1	3	1	2	2	2	1	4	4	-
4) No attempt	2	4	4	2	2	4	8	4	9	7
5) **Non User** Correct	4	1	2	2	2	2	2	2	-	2
6) Correct Context	-	1	-	1	1	1	1	-	-	-
7) Attempted/Incorrect	-	1	-	-	-	-	-	-	2	-
8) No Attempt	1	2	3	2	2	2	2	3	3	3

	23	24	25	26	27	28	29	30	31
1) **User** Correct	1	3	-	-	-	2	4	11	2
2) Correct Context	1	1	-	-	-	5	1	1	2
3) Attempted/Incorrect	9	6	10	7	5	1	1	-	10
4) No attempt	3	4	4	7	9	6	8	2	-
5) **Non User** Correct	-	-	-	-	1	1	2	5	1
6) Correct Context	-	-	-	-	-	-	-	-	1
7) Attempted/Incorrect	3	2	2	2	1	1	-	-	-
8) No Attempt	2	3	3	3	3	3	3	-	2

	32	33	34	35	36	37	38	39	40	41	42	43	44
1) **User** Correct	11	11	12	10	13	13	13	1	1	8	11	6	1
2) Correct Context	1	-	-	-	-	-	-	1	1	3	1	2	2
3) Attempted/Incorrect	-	-	-	3	-	-	-	7	7	1	2	4	5
4) No attempt	2	3	2	1	1	1	1	5	5	2	-	2	6
5) **Non User** Correct	4	4	4	3	4	5	5	1	1	4	4	1	-
6) Correct Context	-	-	-	-	1	-	-	-	-	-	-	1	-
7) Attempted/Incorrect	-	-	-	1	-	-	-	4	4	1	-	1	1
8) No Attempt	1	1	1	1	-	-	-	-	-	-	1	2	4

	45	46	47	48	49	50	51	52	53	54	55	56	57
1) **User** Correct	11	11	12	10	6	6	1	1	1	1	1	-	-
2) Correct Context	-	2	1	1	4	5	3	3	-	1	1	-	-
3) Attempted/Incorrect	2	-	-	-	-	-	2	2	1	1	2	1	1
4) No attempt	1	1	1	3	4	3	8	8	12	11	10	13	13
5) **Non User** Correct	3	3	3	2	1	1	1	1	-	-	-	-	-
6) Correct Context	-	-	-	-	1	1	1	1	-	-	-	-	-
7) Attempted/Incorrect	-	-	-	1	1	1	-	-	-	-	-	-	-
8) No Attempt	2	2	2	2	2	2	3	3	5	5	5	5	5

	58	59	60
1) **User** Correct	-	-	-
2) Correct Context	3	1	-
3) Attempted/Incorrect	-	2	-
4) No attempt	11	11	14
5) **Non User** Correct	-	-	-
6) Correct Context	1	-	-
7) Attempted/Incorrect	-	2	-
8) No Attempt	4	3	5

effects which relate to the 'receiving end' of communication. This can also be true of compound icons learnt through similar systems. McQuail and Windahl go on to say that it will 'also affect the culture, the stock of knowledge, the norms and the values . . . they make available a set of images, ideas and evaluations from which members can draw in choosing their own lines of behaviour'. How this impacts upon user interfaces is through how users perceive events and react. The results of the test indicate that compound icons fall into certain divisions, and that there are certain expectations of what their denotation is. Icon use fell mainly into the categories:

1) Those that have been learned and are understood by both groups having encountered the icon before in that context – the printer can be found in many application programs (figure 1.4).

2) Those that are least understood through little or no use, such as repaginate (figure 1.21).

3) Those that are generally specific to one program, but can be found in other specialist software other than word processing, such as nested paragraphs (figure 1.11).

4) Those that are used in another program with a different connotation, such as 'save', 'software library' 'inserted disc' and so on (figure 1.3).

5) Those that have a greater connotation as something else – most respondents read 'print preview' as 'add picture' (figure 1.25). The test subjects have assigned a meaning with neither group giving a correct response or identifying the context in which it would be used. This compound icon has a higher number of respondents giving a similar incorrect answer.

6) Those that are abstract and have been learned requiring prior knowledge, such as tabulation. Only one test subject appears to use tabulate left, centre and right (figures 1.53 – 1.55), but does not use the decimal tab or vertical line insertion (figures 1.56 – 1.57). All respondents failed to identify the table margin compound icon (figure 1.60).

Individual test subjects who used Microsoft Word as their primary word processing software were asked about their understanding of the compound icons used. The first category of icons have been learned through user preference – this can be considered as their usual routine of using the program. Comprehension of the compound icons reflect the test subject's use of the program to achieve a task. Primary events show user comprehension, such as creating new documents, saving, printing, spell checking, making style changes to the type and so on. There was free admission that to perform tasks which are not part of the user's normal routine, other methods were used. For example, nested and unnested paragraph compound icons were rarely used, and of those that did nest paragraphs, it was achieved by using 'pidgin' discourse by using the tab key or the word space bar to create the desired outcome. Of those that understood and used nested paragraphs in the correct context, denotation was learnt through www software where the compound icon is similar for nesting and unnesting and is regularly used (figures 1.10 and 1.11).

As described in the previous chapter, investment in learning appears to be through the incentive to gain something through use of a program, or as McQuail and Windahl (ibid, p.19) state, the 'transactional' way of looking at perception. McQuail and Windahl then go on to state that 'human communication process may be regarded as subjective, selective, variable and unpredictable and that human communication systems are open systems'. This partly explains why only one person adjusted the tabulation points (figures 1.53 to 1.55), instead of using the preset tab key default spaces. Individuals were staying within the parts of the program metaphor that allowed them to perform a task and no more. These 'events' appear to have been learnt and used in the correct context. Other sub-goals functions were achieved by other means, or simply not used and this is true of both groups. As described with the tab key or space bar to achieve tabulation, perception of an event might be carried out through a reaction that is commonly used in one form until the correct use of a compound icon is understood.

McQuail and Windahl identified George Gerbner's general model of communication as having a wide range of applications. The adaption of the verbal model would be:

the user of a program

perceives an event

and reacts

in one form

in that context

with some consequence

Gerbner's general model is then graphically sub-divided to allow for the inclusion of intentionality which is important for human-computer or human-computer-human interaction because it suplements context and possible consequence. Aaron Marcus (1984, p.365-378) writes that by establishing a universal visual language 'with consistent meaning throughout the interface' spatial memory can be aided by separating out functionality, combined with a consistent design approach uniformly adopted for the development of programs for computers. Therefore, by learning one application users already know how other applications will possibly work. The Apple computer interface recognised this, for example the menu bar remains consistent between programs – the Apple, File and Edit are always located to the left of the bar, further additions to the menu bar are specific to the program. At all times users have a familiar reference point. As a metaphor the menu that can be 'pulled down' shares no resemblance with its original restaurant counterpart. By having this abstract association with its original it separates functionality from representative compound icons providing the choice of action after the compound icon (or single paradigm of operation, for example text edit and so on) has been selected (see Chapter 1). Navigation becomes icon selection and available action/verb. Non-applicable actions are denied users, the action/verb becomes 'greyed-out'. Computer navigation within a program expands the primary desktop metaphor encouraging users to 'see-and-point' and, as stated earlier by Apple, human-computer interaction should be 'hey, you – do this' (figure 2). Therefore, interfaces should be consistent across all computer platforms.

Figure 2. For computer interfaces Gerbner's general model is sub-divided (reproduced from British American Tobacco pitch graphics).

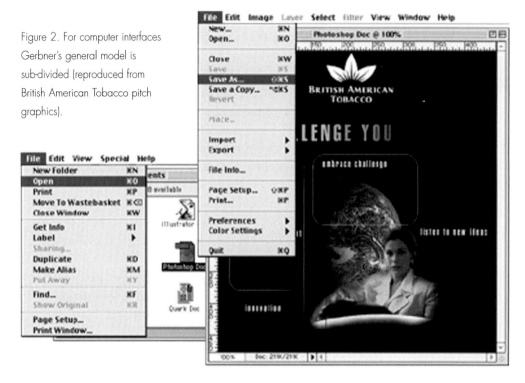

a) Navigation becomes icon selection

b) Non-applicable actions are denied the user

Anthony Wetherell (1978, p.324.-328) considers that spatial memory can be disrupted if processing one set of information interferes with the 'processing of a prior set (retroactive inhibition), especially when the two sets are in similar formats', and that 'memory for graphic information is in some way different from memory for verbal information'. An analogy would be to change the position of the clock in your house from one location to another, then recount how many times your eye returns to the old familiar location. There may be good reasons to move the clock. Bruce Tognazzini (1978, p.76-77) identifies two points of consistency to stabilise a system where the entire look and feel of a program has been changed. '1) Consistent interpretation of user behaviour by the system is more important than consistent system objects and behaviours . . . 2) If you must make a change, make it a large and obvious one'. Simply put by him, honour the user's previously learned sense of location by not shuffling all the toolbox icons around when new ones are created, because this disrupts spatial memory. Spatial memory was more disruptive during the upgrade phase from Photoshop 3 to 4, (figure 3a) and less disruptive during the upgrade of QuarkXPress 3 to 4, even though there is a seven year gap between the QuarkXPress upgrade (spatial disruption was included in the beta test cycle of QuarkXPress 4, 1996-97) (figure 3b).

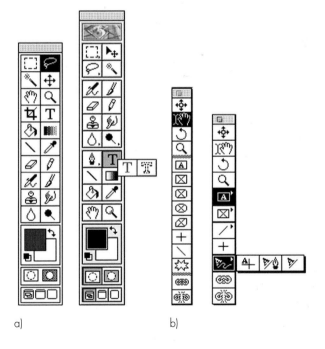

a)   b)

Figure 3. Toolboxes from different application programs a) Photoshop 3, and Photoshop 4 b) QuarkXPress 3, and QuarkXPress 4 (reproduced from Adobe Photoshop and QuarkXPress interfaces).

Unlike the ARC questionnaire discussed in the last chapter, the data at the beginning of this chapter does not test the user's ability to acquire a lexicon, but does require information retrieved from long-term memory as stated by Card, Moran and Newell (1983, p.10) the 'Discrimination Principle' of other similar items in memory that might have a different denotation, and are 'more sensitive to semantic interference (they are confused with other items with similar meaning)'. John Foley (1993, p.129) writes that semantic interference during the 'Wars of the Roses' changed English history. 'Forces of the Yorkist king Edward IV, bearing the royal badge of the "Sun in Splendour", a sun with rays, encountered the Lancastrian forces led by the Earl of Warwick . . . on Warwick's side was De Vere, the Earl of Oxford, whose soldiers bore the the "Estoile", a star and rays'. By mistaking the denotation of a star at night for brilliant sunshine Warwick attacked his own side giving Edward the victory. Through the questionnaire semantic interference is apparent when compound icons are used with different connotations in other programs. Both sun and star were abstract symbols and require prior knowledge to make a distinction if semantic interference is to be avoided.

Otto Neurath (1980, p.20) suggests that 'reading a picture language is like making observations with the eye in everyday experience', real world representation through illustration has more power to convey complex ideas by being selective of what is included within the image. The effectiveness of this interface combination is what it has selectively decided to tell us, and, therefore, what designers has consciously omitted. For example, according to Yukio Ota, (1993, p.109) Yamashita's designs for the Tokyo Olympic Games and the Sapporo Winter Olympic Games were influenced by Neurath. Yamashita tells Ota that he 'was entranced by Neurath's Isotype, I was entrusted with the work of designing the event symbols . . . sign design consists of eliminating all unnecessary things'. Aaron Marcus (1984, p.368) wrote 'that corporate graphics implies that attention is given to the unique communication needs of all images, but at the same time the images are adjusted to produce a visual consistency . . . to establish recognizability, clarity and consistency just as verbal or linguistic techniques are applied to the text to promote simplicity, clarity, familiarity, integrity and consistency'. The simpler and more graphically averaged an image element is, the easier it is to remember. For example, the idealised representation of a maple leaf used on the Canadian flag is graphically refined to visually average all features of that leaf, and therefore, represent all maple leaves (figure 4). The homepages of the Maple Leaf Language Academy (1998) and the Vancouver Tourist Guide (1998) (figure 5) would be better at describing a specific place and not an overall representation of place like eWorld (figure 7, later).

Maple Leaves　　　　Canadian Flag　　　　　　　　　Computer Icon

Figure 4. Maple leaves and the Maple leaf visually averaged to represent all Maple leaves used on the Canadian Flag (Internet, 30th August 1998) (reproduced from the Canadian Clip Art Library).

Figure 5. Images that are photographic are better at describing a particular place, a) The Maple Leaf Language Academy, and b) Tourist Guide to Vancouver.

a)　　　　　　　　　　　　　　　b)

Magazines can mix these approaches and help the reader to navigate content. In this respect they are similar to websites where progress is non-linear – readers are not expected to start at the beginning and continue until finished like reading a novel in a book. Magazine pages might contain different information centred on a specific theme, but requiring some form of distinction, for example the main article could discuss a new processor. Amongst or surrounding the article is other information that compares the different system processors and their speeds. Sections might be different from each other and will require some graphic device to signal the distinction. Therefore visual strategies are used by magazine designers to allow the reader to leave, look about, acquire additional information, compare and then possibly return. The magazine *MacUser* demonstrates the importance of this and displays the navigational technique of how this is achieved. How this was implemented when it was redesigned in 1994, and what further changes took place up to 1997 prove to be of value when demonstrating this process.

Magazines are not arbitrary designs each has a perception of its readership and how the reader can best be informed through the application of design and editorial content. People read magazines aligned to their interests, how the magazine presents itself reflects the readership, and in this respect many corporate websites are no different in how they go about attracting target users . The publisher knows the profile of its readership and how they can attract an audience through the application of design. One good example among many is the United Kingdom redesign of *MacUser* launched on 22 July 1994. The new look of the magazine included the Officina type family designed by Erik Spiekermann which is a sans serif monoweight with square serif overtones. Frutiger has many variations, and because of this, was choosen for the primary typography. Visage was again brought by *MacUser* especially for the redesign. Three families used together require a critical understanding of typography. Certain parts of the magazine went untouched. The *MacUser* logo was kept the same, to retain the brand image which had already been established. It was the design of the magazine that changed and not the contents, the same sections appeared in the same places throughout the magazine. Again this would have been done so as not to totally alienate regular readers. With the change a certain amount of familiarity had to be maintained. *MacUser's* brief for the redesign was:

> to modernise the look of *MacUser*, but . . . the constraints placed [upon us] were to do this while maintaining a similar word count in most sections, to maintain clarity . . . and to make the same budget do more. We also had to ensure the design would work within a fort-nightly production schedule (Williams, 1994).

Obviously during that period the senior art director Matt Williams, and his team were aware that a large part of *MacUser's* readership are people who are involved in design themselves and in producing magazines and other materials on Macintosh computers so they were, 'redesigning to a critical audience, many of whom know as much as we do'. The three major areas of the redesign were in structure, the compound icons and typography. The new structure has a header that appears at the start of articles that is directly related to the front cover. The contents page has changed quite dramatically. The new design makes it easier to locate different sections of the magazine and that is, first and foremost, the main objectives of a contents page. Raymond Pirouz and Lynda Weinman (1997, p.94) state that for websites navigational compound icons should be 'bundled together in an easy-to-comprehend manner', they should also be a high priority in that pages reading order. *MacUser's* family range of compound icons are colour coded, which helps to keep the relevant areas together, and also helps the reader to distinguish certain sections when looking through the magazine adding identity and continuity to the pages. However, the redesign retained certain characteristics of previous icons, keeping a certain amount of consistency and familiarity with previous issues, so the reader was not required to relearn a system – merely adapt to the new (figure 6). The

change has been in the design of the pages and navigation of
the content, there are no new sections and the positions of the
headers have remained in the same order in relation to each
other, but have moved down to the lower half of the page. This
again is part of the familiarity that regular readers can associate with the 'old' *MacUser*.

a) Money matters   b) Design matters   c) Mac solutions   d) System essentials

Figure 6. 1994 family of *MacUser* compound icons (reproduced from *MacUser*).

With the 1997 edition of *MacUser* the icons have a loose connection with visual language, their connotation is through
association with the first illustration that features at the beginning of the article, and will change from issue to issue. David
Canter (1978, p.253-254) writes that 'in identifying a location
the task is to represent what the location is by reference to some
knowledge which the individual can already assume to have'.
The content of the article concerns updating from MacOS 7 to
MacOS 8 and has an introductory illustration by Rian Hughes
(1997, p.80-81) (figure 7). The illustration is of a silhouette of a
male and female around a monitor which contains the caption
inside the monitor 'are you compatible?'. The icon used
throughout the article comes from a part of that illustration
(figure 8a). This icon is repeated at the starting point of the
article on each page, because pages throughout the article
contain other relevant information (figure 9). This is similar to
the purpose of sub-headings or computer icons that serve an
associative purpose as an arrival point which allows the reader
to navigate directly to a starting or continuation point; causes a
change of page colouration allowing the reader to look away,
and return with little effort; and informs the reader of the following content (figure 8).

148

a) Software update

b) Colour scanning

c) Web software

Figure 8. All article icons are used as a point of continuation. This has the advantage of allowing the reader to leave, look about, acquire additional information, compare and then possibly return to that point (reproduced from *MacUser*).

Figure 7. 1997 *MacUser* icons have an implied connection with the content, their denotation is through association with the first illustration that features at the beginning of each article (reproduced from *MacUser*).

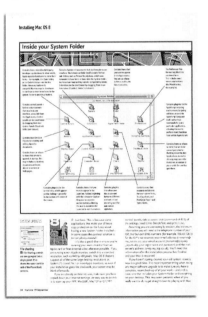

Figure 9. The icon is repeated at the continuation point of the article on all subsequent pages linking content, this is because pages throughout the article contain other relevant information (reproduced from *MacUser*).

MacUser also uses colour to assist navigation, in a similar way to underground maps that also successfully rely upon coloured lines and place names. Regular commuters of underground systems understand their route. Visitors, or that same commuter choosing a different route will need to consult the underground map to find out what is required. The regular user does not need to learn how the map works, it is simply a case of applying what they already know. Also the system has been adopted by underground networks worldwide, therefore that same user can understand how to navigate around other countries' cities. Combining Harry Beck's (Green and Rewse-Davis, 1995, p.74) system with icons can aid user navigation within systems that have functionality as part of the final destination rather than a place location.[2] Other systems of navigation such as the signage routes used for a large multi-national hotel and leisure complex can also learn from Beck who deliberately edited out information that is usually associated with maps. During 1982 the Corinthia Group of Companies completed the building of the Jerma Palace Hotel at Marsacala Bay in Malta. The 350 room hotel and leisure complex was designed to be used by tourists mainly from England, France, Germany, Italy and from Arab speaking countries. One of the major problems for a navigational sign system within the complex was the removal of written language. Computer interfaces can change basic words according to the language of users. Yet the signs need underpinning with written language at some point if the user is to learn the system. Of this Neurath (1980, p.16) writes that a picture language is not able to give the story by itself, 'but only with the help of words of a normal language'.

Inside the Jerma Palace all starting points are not from the reception, but from the guests room and at selected points, such as the stair wells where the lifts are located. The rooms contain a 'menu' leaflet with the basic key words, for example, Freibad, Pont de Piscine and Ponte Piscina underpin the Pool Deck symbol. Key basic words for western languages present little problem. However, it was difficult to find some basic words in Arabic, such as bar and pool bar. The stair wells contain the

[2] The first London Underground folding pocket map was issued in 1908 and followed a geographically correct positioning in relation to the street map. As the system grew the network of tube lines expanded into the suburbs it became increasingly difficult to continue with a geographically accurate version. In 1931 Harry Beck proposed a design that was based upon an electrical circuit diagram, to show relationships but not their scale.

lifts and are a natural pause in a person's journey, containing five hexagonal 'menu' panels, one for each language. After the basic word has been identified with the symbol, all further sign panels contain no words only symbols. Web browsers allow the user to show the tool bar as either pictures, text, or pictures and text. Choice of how the interface appears depends upon an individual's familiarity with that browser and can be customised accordingly. The hotel system cannot adjust according to user comprehension, but it can remove text from the symbol during the journey, so users are expected to make destination decisions and simply follow the route colour, using the symbols as memory prompts.

Activities are grouped into colour coded areas along the hotel route. Once the symbol for that colour group is known, users then follow the appropriate colour, such as blue, red, green, yellow, black or white which form interlocing hexagons.[3] This principle is similar to Harry Beck's 1931 underground map, i.e. your destination is on the yellow line, once on you simply need to know when to get off, or join another route.[4] Depending on where the user is within the complex, determines the availability of navigational target colour along the route (figure 10). This is to give the user an idea of distance from the final location and availability of other locations on different route hexagons. Evelyn Goldsmith (1984, p.403) writes that 'if speed is the main criterion in a search task, then of all the coding devices available colour seems to be the most successful'. Aaron Marcus (1992, p.82) considers that a 'maximum of five plus or minus two' distinct colours are appropriate as 'this amount allows extra room in short-term memory'. With the hotel this was the main purpose of the navigation system, icons are then used as prompts to change routes. Websites also use some of these principles for navigation to varing degrees. Peter Kentie (1997, p.17) states that the user should be able 'to jump from one page to another regardless of level', but with the ever increasing complexity of some corporate websites it is only a sense of distance between the different section that can only really be maintained. The centre in the hotel model is the

[3] The target array colours were chosen after colour blindness tests during the development of the sign system, after the absolute primaries red, green and blue, boundaries between red and green create yellow, and white mixes all wheras black mixes nothing. After RGB and yellow, distinction between colour tends to merge at the wavelength boundaries.

[4] The first underground maps were not issued until 1933, because of extensive testing.

location of the user, and any interface such as a website should give the user a sense of distance between places by reordering the locations or by key routes available from any location.

Like the hotel navigation system, good websites will normally have different areas of activity, and like the hotel which physically contains all these activities a website gives a sense of being contained through graphics, colour and when present, icons designed as a family. It is simpler to think of a website as the hotel analogy, or a network of connecting locations with different functions within one building, connecting to other related buildings and so on. Apple's eWorld (online information and communication service) might not have had the take-up it deserved and the reasons for its lack of popular success have nothing to do with the principles behind its design.[5] eWorld used the metaphor of a town where users experience eWorld in the same way that they would interact with a real world town. Therefore, if the computer desktop metaphor is globally consistent, and only the written languages change for the user's country, then many dispersed groups can communicate through those same metaphors.

Interfaces that use Real World Metaphors

If the buildings in eWorld were photographic like the home-pages of the The Maple Leaf Language Academy and the Vancouver Tourist Guide, eWorld's interface would be better at describing a specific place, which would be alienating to users who do not physically live at the location of the photographs, (figure 5, earlier). When a connection has been made to eWorld the user will see the pictorial interpretation of idealised buildings in the town square. These buildings represent connections to services that can be found in such places as the Arts & Leisure Pavilion, Business & Finance Plaza, Learning Centre, Marketplace and so on (figure 11). Buildings like the Community Centre contain different categories of compound icon. Knowledge of how navigation works for individuals should not be assumed, as Canter (1978, p.247) writes, 'it is important to recognise, however, that just as people will differ in their

Figure 10. Combinations of hexagons showing navigational choice along a route.

[5] Apple has over 14,000 active technical articles on it's website. Reference to eWorld has been largely removed but is occasionally still referenced, such as article 20231 which discusses modems and was last modified on 26th August 96, 'page 11. disregard the reference to eWorld', although it is still a registered trademark. Apple (Internet). Downloaded from the www 31st March 1999. http://www.apple.com

degree of disorientation for any given location, places vary in the amount of "lostness" they engender' and as Kentie (1997, p.165) makes clear that 'people have been known to get lost within a single website'. Darrell Sano (1996, p.86) who is an interface designer with the Netscape Communication Corporation considers that 'inadequate visual clues and convoluted pathways through the information space contribute most to that feeling of disorientation'. eWorld recognises this and breaks down the interface into manageable areas through the metaphor of buildings, and different kinds of compound icon once entered. By categorising the compound icons, their context helps to supply the knowledge to redress disorientation. These interface compound icons fall into three distinct categories:

1) Place – where the user is within the site.
2) Content – what kind of information.
3) Function – what the user can do.

Figure 11. The eWorld interface (reproduced from eWorld).

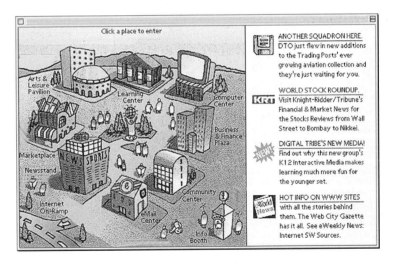

For example, the Auditorium place icon found inside the Community Centre will allow the user to interact with other connected users. Everything there describes events in the real world such as seminars, meetings, and training courses (figure 12). Like an auditorium in use there will also be hundreds, if not thousands of other participants, and like any theatre the user can sit with a row of people, and see the text that they type. The user can exchange text with other rows or individuals by name and may also interact with special guests who are appearing on the stage. Each building will contain activities that their real-world counterpart would have such as the arts, television, hobbies, games, shareware libraries, publications, live role playing, financial information, financial news, industry-specific information and so on.

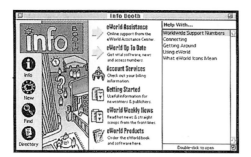 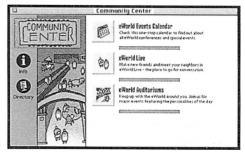

Figure 12. Inside the buildings the layout for each screens content is the same ensuring that there is no spatial disruption when locating places, content or functions (reproduced from eWorld).

Most of eWorld activities are through some form of transaction or interaction. During the ARC research programme 56% of communication was between shared screen and real-time text exchange between different language groups. For groups that spoke the same language only 27% of communication was through shared screen and real-time text exchange (Honeywill *et al*, 1995). The opposite was true for shared screen and simultaneous sp-phone, this suggests that users with English as a second language prefer to supplement communication with text. By using the same language both groups can understand the semantics and pragmatics of what is being communicated only at their level of language competence. It is the visual metaphor for a location and its content that addresses overall comprehension, but not the emphatic. Marcus (1999) defines semantic and pragmatics for the GUI as different from other disciplines, semantics address 'the qualities of the visual sign that allow it to represent, or refer to, an object, process, or concept'. The pragmatic dimension refers to the consumption of signs: 'can one read it from a distance of 28" (a typical CRT viewing distance)? Does the sign appeal to the viewer? Does it seem alien or foreign?' Interface semantics and pragmatics can get the user to a destination, the transactional nature for the kind of place and its content is then concerned with the abilities of individuals.

a) Section   b) Conference   c) Auditorium   d) Gateway

Figure 13. Place icons. eWorld makes the transition from systems icons to www icons and still retain the ethos of a 32x32 pixel matrix. (reproduced from Apple eWorld).

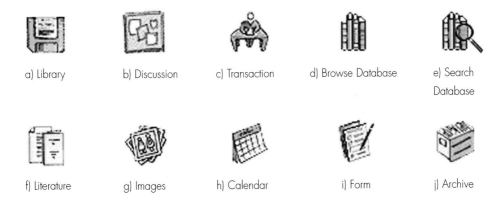

a) Library   b) Discussion   c) Transaction   d) Browse Database   e) Search Database

f) Literature   g) Images   h) Calendar   i) Form   j) Archive

Figure 14. Content icons (reproduced from Apple eWorld).

As pointed out in previous chapters function icons contain general icon elements such as the 'i' for information, '?' for help and the magnifying glass for find. These icon elements can be encountered in other programs and websites normally in that context. They are also distinct from the place and content compound icon categories (figures 13 and 14) which share the same interface location within eWorld. However, the use of icon elements as part of a visual language lexicon can be seen between the Search Database icon magnifying glass element (figure 14e), and the same element used to make a general search (figure 15c). John Morgan and Peter Welton (1986, p.36) write that the definition of 'a sign is any physical entity to which a community attributes meaning'. The icon elements 'i' and '?' can be found in many systems, search or find is less common outside of computer interfaces – it is used on websites from around the world to mean precisely that. As stated, through long term and regular use these icon elements along with a few others, have developed naturally and have gone mainly unquestioned.

The principle of eWorld's use of metaphor as visual language for place, content and function emphasises utility and serves as a reference point for web interfaces long after the original technologies involved are obsolete where language and technology progress at different rates and for different reasons. Pirouz and Weinman (1997, p.5) explain that 'the web is in a constant state of metamorphoses and evolution, outdating itself monthly, weekly, and even daily'. Goldsmith (1984, p.414) identifies 'three levels of image perception: detection, acknowledgement of the existence of an image; recognition, an ability to match the image with an object; and identification, the naming of an image by the subject'. Continual change and redesign is not limited to the web, all good design is in a constant state of flux – change is gradual or innovative, but always constant, and like *MacUser* small amounts of change do not alienate what the end user already knows. Regardless of the change of content or visual 'mood' of a website, how users navigate using visual language should remain constant regardless of a change to an icon's presentation. For example, visual semantics should simply substitute Neurath's 1930s aeroplane for a modern contempory such as those elements used for the website of Singapore Changi International Airport (1999) (figures 16a, 16b and 16c).

a) Information

b) New

c) Find

d) Feedback

e) Help

f) Directory

Figure 15. Function icons (reproduced from Apple eWorld).

a)

b)

EATING AND DRINKING   TRANSIT HOTELS   SCIENCE DISCOVERY CORNER   TRANSFER COUNTER

c)

Figure 16. Similar to MacUser and eWorld's use of compound icons there are changes in style of presentation of compound icons within the same website, but visual language remains constant regardless of a change to their presentation (reproduced from Singapore Changi International Airport website).

The compound icons for Singapore Changi International Airport are not only identifiable for their probable ICAO/UIC (International Committee of Aviation Organisation and Union

International des Chemins de fer) source but also for their corporate intonation, many of which were entered into the ISO directory as a verbal description some decades earlier. Standardisation is difficult to apply for signs and is difficult to regulate therefore the ISO, initiated through the Technical Committee 145, made two decisions according to Harm Zwaga and Ronald Easterby (1978, p.278) the first decision 'was that the standard would be restricted to a verbal description of the image content of the symbol . . . the second decision was that the selection of the standard verbal description of the image content for a symbol should be based upon an evaluation of any proposals to guarantee that the user population would comprehend the symbols'. Many icons have been developed and catalogued yet only a few have been used. The outcome of this is that many large organisations have used these standards to reflect their corporate identity and this can also be true of websites. Many corporate identity manuals still do not reflect the Internet at this point, therefore conventional publication standards are being applied to website design.

The three following web pages are the Photoshop presentation screens created for a Trotman-Online presentation to Lloyds TSB for the graduate recruitment section of their website (figure 17).[6] The three screens are developed according to a series of paper-based guidelines which describe colour, typography, how the logo can and cannot be used, together with what is appropriate for images, and that it should always identify any user with it, with the inclusion of 'you, your or yourself'. This creates a linkage for the website with how Lloyds TSB wish to be perceived. Visuals for website presentations normally take about seven hours to design three screens. Obviously the whole website is considered, but the home screen will inform how the others will be designed and will normally take approximately five hours to design, (figure 17a) the second will take about an hour and a quarter, (figure 17b) and the third about three quarters of an hour. This also includes going back across all three screens to ensure that they reflect the overall design standard that brings them together as one website.

[6] These visuals are combined with a site map to demonstrate functionality, This presentation came second out of the six.

Figure 17. Photoshop presentation screens created for a Trotman-Online pitch to Lloyds TSB for the graduate recruitment section of their website. Iconically, the first screen involves developing navigational icons that will be used on further pages. Like Singapore Changi International Airport many of these icons have already gone through a developmental and testing process through ISO semantic evaluations. Aaron Marcus points out that during 1985 the Xerox Corporation had already made efforts to standardise icons through ISO and ANSI (American National Standards Institute).

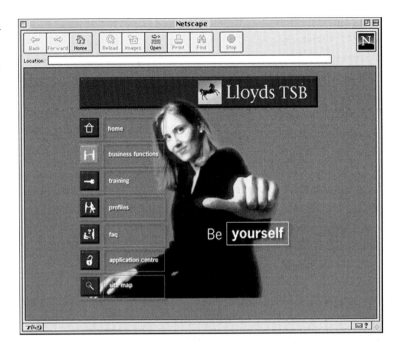

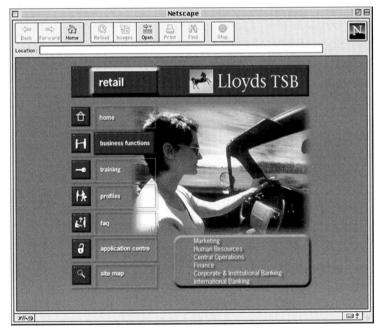

The compound icons themselves are not perfect at the presentation stage. Indeed other companies will also be tendering ideas
and presenting these on the same day. If the website design is
won by Trotman-Online then the design will be finalised and
will include the changing of icons according to the wishes of
Lloyds TSB, and possibly changing the style but not the semantic values that they imply. For example the line weight and style
of two icons which represent home and site map are incorrect
(figure 18a and 18g). While the key is indexical to 'opening
doors' and therefore represents training is visually and mathematically too low within the compound (figure 18c). All other
icons are based upon ISO for either Public Information to navigate through spaces, photography (figure 18f) or the infixed key
element used in Accommodation and Travel (figure 18c). The
compound icon which represents Frequently Asked Questions
on the Lloyds TSB interface (figure 18e) was originally designed
and tested in 1975 by Zwaga and Easterby (1978, p.284) as
one possible referent to information. The results of their com-
prehsion/recognition test placed this icon as the highest
ranking variant for information with 52% responses correct,
with 'i' on its own 35% percent and '?' juxtaposed with another
question mark 47%. The two figures, one sitting and one stand-
ing, help the context of the '?', that there is some form of
exchange of information between the two figures.

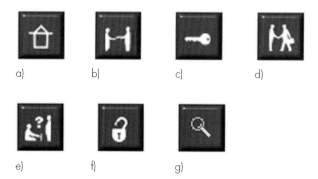

a)   b)   c)   d)

e)   f)   g)

Figure 18. The compound icons themselves are not perfect at the presentation stage
– all elements except g) appear low within the compound icon.

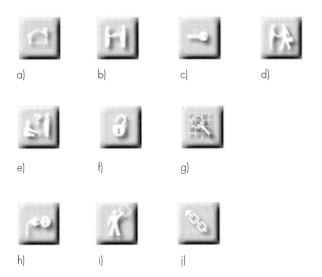

a)　　　　b)　　　　c)　　　　d)

e)　　　　f)　　　　g)

h)　　　　i)　　　　j)

Figure 19. Reusing and refining icons with further icons added to the family range. 18a) and 19b) are still houses, but different styles of house, 18b) represents business function and 19b) represents challenge, in this respect both are similar. 18c) and 19c) are training, 18d) and 19d) are both profiles, whereas 18e) is frequently asked questions and 19e) is information about Post Office recruitment (again these are similar). 18f) is application centre while 19f) is launch your career, which again is the same thing said differently. 18g) looking at an overview of the website, whereas 19g) uses the magnifying glass with a grid infixed into the compound icon to represent how the next page is a grid of Post Office careers. The next three are 19h) application process (plug and socket) 19i) advertisements and campaigns (man waving a paper in the air). Finally 19j) links which is a chain with an arrow.

By adapting icons that were originally intended as navigation but not for computer interfaces, Edward de Bono (1971, p.237) says that it is 'to do with rearranging available information so that it is snapped out of the established pattern and forms a new and better pattern'. Therefore the flow of thinking about what it is that has been perceived and considered as having application and potential is stored away by some degree. This is true of icons used on both Singapore Changi International Airport and Lloyds TSB which refer back to ISO, but also between Singapore Changi International Airport and Lloyds

TSB in how the icons are 'housed' with the text – home, business function and so on. This relationship can then again be seen to develop between icons used for Lloyds TSB and a further reworking and refining with further icons added to the family range for the Post Office (figure 19, page 161). Then there is the influence of 'similarity of purpose'. If one organisation does something that is similar to another, then comparisons will probably be made. For example the briefing document for the design of the Post Office graduate recruitment website cites, two websites that they consider good – both sites are directly related to recruitment. This is not dissimilar to other briefing documents that make comparison regardless of the subject (figure 20). Overall there is a convergence of the concerns of those who commission websites to ensure that something is as good as something else, and is probably true of those who design them. Innovation can happen through the introduction of something which has been stored away and is possibly unrelated at one point, but can be used at the appropriate moment.

To test this hypothesis of influences between related activities further a survey was undertaken of 192 spread across six continents between the period 7 January – 20 April 1999. The search was limited to ISPs (Internet Service Providers) for each country to establish how icons appear on their interfaces and to explore the notion that they do indeed influence each others' development in some form. The reason for choosing ISPs was that many of these companies design websites for other organisations, therefore this influence possibly continues to other parts of the Internet. To logically follow through on these, further connections were considered inappropriate. This was a small-scale investigation which attempts to make some sense of what de Bono (ibid, p.243) considers as something that is recognised 'only after it has brought something about'. de Bono (ibid, p.240) uses an analogy to describe this as being unable to 'plan a new style in art, but once it has come about it creates its own validity'. This also helps to explain why computer compound icons used as interface navigation go unchallenged.

Figure 20. The original
Post Office graduate
recruitment home screen,
where the image used is
not required to mean any-
thing, the 'it's not just
about . . .' link goes
directly to a flash file
which then goes through
a sequence – 'It's not just
about red vans, it's not just
about delivering letters'
and so on.

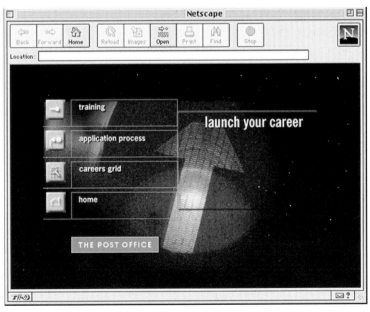

Icons from around the World

The small-scale investigation was limited to Yahoo and to a set sequence, therefore if an ISP was not registered with this search engine then their domain name would not appear. For instance the search result using this criteria for Japan reveals 29 results, yet if the search instruction was altered to 'Japan ISP' then the result would be radically different. The other criteria for the search was that the first entry listed in the Yahoo search result would be the link used to provide the data, also countries with many ISPs scarching was limited to the first 50. Not all service providers have icon-driven interfaces, the average seems to be one in six. Another point to remember is that the amount of registration constantly changes, for example during February 1999 the United Kingdom as a search result was changed from the United Kingdom to its constituent parts of England, Scotland, Northern Ireland and Wales. Some smaller countries had no ISPs while Texas (1310) had twice the provision of the entire Austalasian continent (836). California (2894) was over double the provision of Texas. Therefore America was surveyed by state. The list below identifies three links, the first Internet Services (figure 21a) shows fourteen records for Taiwan; further down the listing are Internet Services, Web Services (figure 21b) with five records which include five ISPs from the first list (figures 21a3, a4, a5, a6 and a8) and finally Internet Services, Web Services, Designers (figure 21c) which contain one record (figures 21a3, b1) which can be also found on the other two links (figure 21).

a) Business and Economy > Companies > **Internet Services** > By Region > Countries > Taiwan

1) BST - FaxNet, Internet dial-up, Internet and Intranet solutions, home page designing, virtual hosts, I-Phone solutions.
2) Chiayu Information Ltd.
3) **E Design** - design, produce, and maintain websites for companies and individuals

Figure 21. a) The higher order of listing contains fourteen search results, five of which can be found in b). c) has only one service provider that can be found on the other two. This indicates the growth pattern of ISPs in Taiwan with the Yahoo search engine.

4) **Evolve New Media** - solutions to your Internet and new media needs.

5) **Greenworld Network Co., Ltd**

6) **I-site Taiwan**

7) Pinho Internet Service Co., Ltd. - offer computer mail order and Internet server technology services.

8) **Starnet Internet Service Corp**.

9) Tainan.com - with news, organizations, and hosting services.

10) Taoyuan Metro - shareware, current events, education, entertainment, and travel news and listings in Chinese.

11) TaoYuan Network - includes information about Taoyuan, electronic shopping, and KiSS.

12) Trace

13) TTN Internet Service

14) Yangyi.com - Chinese-English homepage design & translation. Complete international internet services

b) Business and Economy > Companies > **Internet Services > Web Services** > By Region > Countries > Taiwan

1) **E Design** - design, produce, and maintain websites for companies and individuals

2) Evolve New Media - solutions to your Internet and new media needs.

3) Greenworld Network Co.,Ltd

4) I-site Taiwan

5) Starnet Internet Service Corp.

c) Business and Economy > Companies > **Internet Services > Web Services > Designers** > By Region > Countries > Taiwan

1) **E Design** - design, produce, and maintain websites for companies and individuals

Africa 114 ISPs

Algeria (0), Angola (2), Benin (0), Botswana (0), Burkina (0), Burundi (1), Cameroon (0), Cape Verde Islands (0), Central African Republic (0), Chad (0), Comoros (0), Congo (0), Djibouti (0), Egypt (27), Equatorial Guinea (0), Eritrea (0), Ethiopia (0), Gabon (0), Gambia (0), Ghana (5), Guinea (0), Guinea-Bissau (0), Ivory Coast (0), Kenya (5), Lesotho (0), Liberia (0), Libya (1), Madagascar (1), Malawi (0), Mali (0), Mauritius (2), Mauritania (0), Morocco (3), Mozambique (0), Namibia (6), Niger (0), Nigeria (0), Rwanda (0), Sao Tome and Principle (0), Senegal (0), Seychelles (0), Sierra Leone (0), Somalia (0), South Africa (86), Sudan (0), Swaziland (0), Tanzania (0), Togo (0), Tunisia (0), Uganda (0), Zaire (0), Zambia (1), Zimbabwe (6)

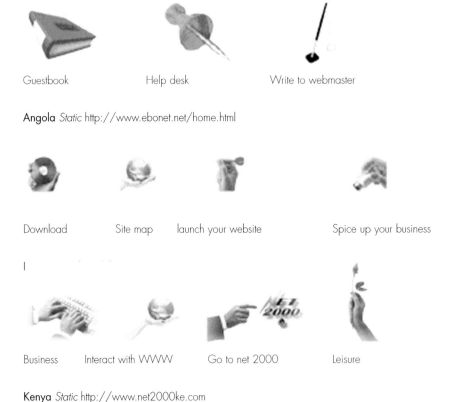

Guestbook   Help desk   Write to webmaster

Angola *Static* http://www.ebonet.net/home.html

Download   Site map   launch your website   Spice up your business

Business   Interact with WWW   Go to net 2000   Leisure

Kenya *Static* http://www.net2000ke.com

About us   Chat   Feedback   Search   Sitemap   Market

South Africa *Static* http://www.os2.iaccess.za

Connections   Contact info   Support   Home   Services and Rates

South Africa *Dynamic* http://www.pe.co.za/index2.htm

About us   Chat   Feedback   Search   Sitemap

Namibia *Static* http://www.iafrica.com.na

Web design   Email   Search   Network Internet Solutions

Zimbabwe *Static* http://www.icon.co.zw

167

Asia 1004 ISPs

Afghanistan (0), Bahrain (2), Bangladesh (10), Bhutan (0), Brunei (1), Cambodia (2), China (229), India (197), Indonesia (34), Iran (0), Iraq (0), Israel (42), Hong Kong (77), Japan (29), Jordan (6), Kazakhstan (1), Kirgyzstan (0), Kuwait (0), Laos (0), Lebanon (12), Malaysia (31), Maldives (0), Mongolia (0), Myanmar (if no try Burma) (0), Nepal (2), North Korea (0), Oman (0), Pakistan (21), Philippines (51), Qatar (0), Russia (29), Saudi Arabia (5), Singapore (131), South Korea (13), Sri Lanka (4), Syria (0), Taiwan (14), Tajikistan (0), Thailand (40), Turkmenia (0), United Arab Emirates (16), Uzbekistan (1), Vietnam (4), Yemen (1).

China *Static* http://www.vtech.net

India *Static* http://www.karnataka.com/megha/

Israel *Static* http://www.zahav.net.il

Lebanon *Dynamic* http://www.netways.com.lb

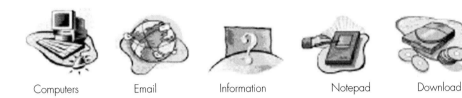

Computers   Email   Information   Notepad   Download

Indonesia *Static* http://www.medan-link.com

Malaysia *Static* http://www.myartists.com/gv/

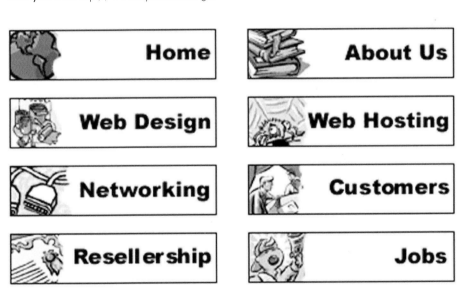

Pakistan *Static* http://www.mags.net.pk/

About us   Clients   Contact us   Email   Faq

Hosting   Members   Sign up   Web page

Philippines *Static* http://www.filbiznet.com

Search   Dial in   People   Russian network

Russia *Static* http://www.komitex.ru

about us | search | contact us | download | sitemap | sitetour

Product & Services   Pricelist   Member's Privilege   Node & Phone Numbers   Member Support   Account Management

Thailand *Static* http://www.loxinfo.co.th

Australasia 886 ISPs

Australia (683), Fiji (6), Kiribati (0), Nauru (0), New Zealand (187), Papua New Guinea (6), Solomon Islands (0), Tonga (2), Tuvalu (1), Vanuatu (0), Western Samoa (1).

Info

Links

News

Search

Internet help

Australia *Static* http://aardvark.apana.org.au

Contact

Home

Links

News

Australia *Dynamic* http://www.at.com.au

Consulting

Design

Hosting

Portfolio

Resources

Fiji *Dynamic* http://www.InternetFiji.com

Information

Contact us

Online

News

Services

New Zealand *Static* http://www.dtl.co.nz

Tonga *Dynamic* http://www.tonic.to

Many ISPs might not know of the existence of others, if there was no transactional need, either through competition or otherwise. However, there is a tentative link, Pakistan (www.mags.net.pk) is aware of Canada (www.racsa.co.cr), while Egypt (http://brainy1.ie-eg.com) is aware of Kenya (www.net2000ke.com) each use icon elements from the other. This suggests a common culture which is shared through computer networks, and because of this as pointed out by web development companies in both Korea and America, many objects and their actions become familiar to all. All can now experience the same information shared through a common interface, therefore the World Wide Web can no longer be con-sidered as a channel of communication alone, but converges into a technology of culture, or culture technology.

Europe 1325 ISPs

Albania (0), Andorra (1), Armenia (5), Austria (34), Azerbaijan (5), Belgium (29),
Belarus (4), Bosnia-Herzegovina (0), Bulgaria (8), Croatia (1), Cyprus (14), Czech
Republic (5), Denmark (21), Estonia (6), Finland (7), France (51), Georgia (3),
Germany (147), Greece (23), Hungary (7), Iceland (9), Irish Republic (0), Italy (300),
Latvia (7), Liechtenstein (2), Lithuania (9), Luxembourg (13), Macedonia (7), Malta
(17), Moldova (0), Monaco (4), Netherlands (169), Norway (14), Poland (17),
Portugal (27), Romania (24), San Marino (1), Slovakia (4), Slovenia (2), Spain (206),
Sweden (29), Switzerland (41), Turkey (26), Ukraine (26),

Chat   Forum   Links   Search

Andorra *Static* http://www.andornet.ad

Ftp   Homepages   Information   Search

Austria *Static* http://www.vip.at

home   About us   Links   Pages   Prices

Bulgaria *Dynamic* http://www.netbg.com

| home | Advice | Contact Form | Contact | Design Service | Email |

| Hosting | Information | Introductions | Links | Search | Snail mail |

Cyprus *Dynamic* http://infowebNET.com/index1.htm

General Information   Products

Denmark *Static* http://www.fenestra.dk

actualité   contact   particuliers   recherche   revendeurs

France *Static* http://www.pandemonium.fr/pandemonium.html

Home   Cool Links   Cool Projects   Email   Wir über uns

Germany *Static* http://www.global.de/global/ga/who1a.html

Whats new   Hardware   Hosting   About us   Random

Italy *Static* http://www.alet.it/2.it/homepage.html

174

Art

Webserver stats

User pages

Ftp

Electronic pages

Ukraine *Static* http://www.lep.lugansk.ua

Information

Contact us

Search

Switzerland *Static* http://www.quaras.ch

Europe - United Kingdom 702 ISPs

England (633), Northern Ireland (16), Scotland (40), Wales (13).

England *Dynamic* http://www.advantage-rt.co.uk

Email form

Home

Northern Ireland *Static* http://www.pmworkshop.co.uk

North America excluding USA 1590 ISPs

Antigua & Barbuda (2), Bahamas (5), Barbados (6), Belize (4), Canada (1338), Costa Rica (21), Cuba (0), Dominica (0), Dominican Republic (16), El Salvador (9), Greenland (0), Grenada (0), Guatemala (8), Haiti (3), Honduras (9), Jamaica (3), Mexico (144), Nicaragua (6), Panama (10), Puerto Rico (0), St. Kitts-Nevis (0), St. Lucia (0), St.Vincent &The Grenadines (0), Trinidad and Tobago (6).

About us

Contact us

What's new

Alliances

Canada *Static* http://www.racsa.co.cr

Internet

Manuals

News

Opinion

Services

Costa Rica *Static* http://www.racsa.co.cr

Children

Company Information

Contact us

home

Members only

National Guide

News

Search

Select sites

Services

Software

Tourism

Guatemala *Static* http://www.infovia.com.gt/indexfr.htm

About us

Clients

Net services

Hardware sales

Software

Tech support

IT support

Technology online

Jamaica *Static* http://www.digtechinc.com

Culture

Events

Ideas

Sites of interest

Mexico *Static* http://eureka.tamnet.com.mx

Culture

Education

Finances

Information

Internal organisation

Items for sale

Medicine

Professional

Services

Software & qualifications

Nicaragua *Static* http://www.ibw.com.ni

United States of America 15,419 ISPs

Alabama (119), Alaska (58), Arizona (265), Arkansas (50), California (2894), Colorado (340), Connecticut (182), Delaware (31), Florida (987), Georgia (516), Hawaii (85), Idaho (69), Illinois (624), Indiana (204), Iowa (94), Kansas (83), Kentucky (74), Louisiana (128), Maine (76), Maryland (362), Massachusetts (571), Michigan (346), Minnesota (384), Mississippi (51), Missouri (223), Montana (58), Nebraska (69), Nevada (118), New Hampshire (88), New Jersey (411), New Mexico (89), New York (897), North Carolina (339), North Dakota (19), Ohio (400), Oklahoma (108), Oregon (310), Pennsylvania (426), Rhode Island (45), South Carolina (114), South Dakota (27), Tennessee (175), Texas (1310), Utah (122), Vermont (34), Virginia (481), Washington (645), Washington DC (0) (comes under Washington), West Virginia (33), Wisconsin (235), Wyoming (23)

ABOUT US   WHAT'S NEW   SUPPORT   CONTACT US

Florida *Static* http://www.javahausweb.com/nhome.htm

Nebraska *Static* http://adnet.net

Company Info   Products   Projects

New Hampshire *Dynamic* http://www.atypica.com

About us   Contact us   Email us   Services   Support

New York *Static* http://www.ythis.com

Search

Oregon *Static* http://www.teleport.com/~avfx/

Home   Our Agency   Portfolio   Results   Teamwork   What's New

Rode Island *Static* http://americahouse.com

Clients   Contact us   Home   About us   Web work

South Carolina *Static* http://www.9voltnet.com

Info   Services   Search   Contact

Texas *Dynamic* http://www.creativeinnovations.com

Client sites   Email   Flash quote   Marketing   Our mission

Wisconsin *Dynamic* http://www.bytesites.com

South America 537 ISPs

Argentina (96), Bolivia (8), Brazil (340), Chile (19), Colombia (19), Ecuador (15), French Guiana (0), Guyana (3), Paraguay (7), Peru (16), Suriname (0), Uruguay (3), Venezuela (11).

Ftp   Ideas   Links   News

Brazil *Static* http://www.bluenet.com.br

Figure 22. Icons from different ISPs from around the world.

As mentioned this is only a small-scale investigation and does not begin to fully tackle the enormity of the task of measuring the development of natural language used throughout the Internet. What is immediately apparent at the time of this survey is that the largest amount of ISPs are spread throughout the United States of America with an overall lower concentration of services providers in the southern and mid-western states, although Texas appears to be the exception to this rule being the second largest state service provider. Overall the United States of America has at this point in time 15,419 ISPs which is just over two and a half time greater than the provision for the rest of the world. Of the English speaking countries, USA has 15,419, UK has 702, Australia has 683, New Zealand has 187 and South Africa has 86, including Canada (although it's French speaking citizens must be taken into account), of the 21,577 servers in recorded use at this point only 3,162 were potentially for non-English use, although English appears to be a dominant factor of these ISPs. Africa has the least provision with 114 ISPs of which 86 are from South Africa and have been included in the English speaking account. Size does not necessarily reflect quality both aesthetically or semantically. The

United States of America might have the largest global provision, yet small countries such as Costa Rica, Zimbabwe or even Nicaragua appear to rival or better American provision, but empirical proof will take extensive research beyond the scope of this book.

Conclusion

Learning how to navigate through a program or a website is through the incentive to make a gain whether it is to word process, layout a desktop published page or navigate to content that is of value. In this sense interaction is subjective and therefore variable according to individual need – the 'transactional' way of looking at perception. Also, the questionnaire identifies that compound icon recognition falls into several categories all of which require prior knowledge, but even prior knowledge and context merely alters the degree of disorientation according to the individual. Icons that do not rely upon prior knowledge can be associated with content and location through exposure to visual information before the user begins, these icons then become specific to that sites content. Underground maps guide the user to their choice of destination, and standardisation of underground maps around the world helps user navigation through long term memory.

Compound icons are not standardised and can be disruptive through semantic interference if the overall denotation has been assigned a different meaning beforehand in a different program and context. Although the Internet is in a constant state of change, if an interface is to be understood long after the technologies involved in its creation are obsolete, computer compound icons should retain natural and not forced elements in their construction, unless perception through transaction is extended by additional functionality. Broken Black letter with rhombic serifs used for the Gutenberg Bible would have been legible to all that could read at that time through familiarity and reinforcement. Textura (the prototype used) now seems illegible to most, however the letters still have the same semantic values, it is merely their presentation that has changed.

Finally, once graphic elements have taken meaning and are used on websites they are possibly redesigned to reflect that website. This is more apparent with corporate websites where the appearance of the website comes first making compound icons subordinate to the identity standards of an organisation. The Post Office buttons and backgrounds can only be chosen from a range of approved colours and this is the same for other corporate websites.

What these icon elements actually are appear to be similar to other websites, also general word usage like 'contact us', 'about us', 'search' and so on appear to be a common standard. This is clearly demonstrated through ISPs from around the world, but there are then icons and natural language that are specific to ISPs. This will also be probably true (speculation untested) for other groups of Internet communities. Neurath was quick to recognise the value of what Ogden was actually doing with written words that were unambiguous, this together with what de Bono recognises is that development is not necessarily through a plan to change or start a trend. This is probably very true of website interfaces because there is very little in the form of organisation outside of W3C (World Wide Web Consortium) that suggests standards, although many symbols recommended by ISO could easily be reappraised for a different navigational context. Further more, even ISO recognised that companies and even countries have preferences. Website interface semantic development appears to be through a subconscious observation of what others do, possibly to ensure that what has been done is no worse than anything else that they themselves might do, with the occasional intervention of other sources that might provide innovation. Therefore natural language that is both written and iconic develops through communities of users each possibly adding their specific use of visual language to the lexicon which also appears to include the words that underpin them.

Bibliography

Albarn, K., Miall-Smith, J., 1977, *Diagram: the instrument of thought*, Thames and Hudson.

Alchemy (Internet). Downloaded from the WWW 15 October 1998 http://www.symbols.com

Apple, 1987, *Human Interface Guidelines: The Apple Desktop Interface*, Addison-Wesley, Massachusetts.

Apple (Internet). Downloaded from the WWW 31 March 1999. http://www.apple.com

Apple, 1988, *Programmer's Introduction to the Apple IIGS*, Addison-Wesley, Massachusetts.

Armstrong, D., Stokoe, W., Wilcox, S., 1995, *Gesture and the Nature of Language*, CUP.

Artillion (Internet). Downloaded from the WWW 20 October 1998. www.artillion.com

Baecker, R., Small, I., 1990, *Animation at the Interface*, Addison-Wesley.

Barnard, P., Marcel, T., 1978, Representation and understanding in the use of symbols and pictograms, R. Easterby, H. Zwaga (eds), *Information Design*, John Wiley and Sons.

Bliss, C., 1965, *Semantography (Blissymbolics)*, 2nd Edition, Semantography (Blissymbolics) Publications, Sydney.

BP Petrol Stations (Internet). Downloaded from the WWW 19 November 1998. http://www.bp.com

Braffort, A., 1997, ARGo: An Architecture for Sign Language Recognition and Interpretation, P. Harling, A. Edwards (eds), *Progress in Gestural Interaction: Proceedings of Gesture Workshop '96*, Springer-Verlag.

Brennan, S., 1990, Conversation as Direct Manipulation: An Iconoclastic View, B. Laural (ed), *The Art of Human-Computer Interface Design*, Addison-Wesley, Massachusetts.

British Steel email briefing document, forwarded by Trotman-Online 26 April 1999.

Burlington Northern Santa Fe (Internet). Downloaded from the WWW 3 May 1999. http://www.bnsf.com

Buxton, B., 1990, The "Natural" Language of Interaction: A Perspective on Nonverbal Dialogues, B. Laural (ed), *The Art of Human-Computer Interface Design*, Addison-Wesley, Massachusetts.

Canadian Flag Clip Art Gallery (Internet). Downloaded from the WWW 30 August 1998 http://members.xoom.com/canfag

Canter, D., 1978, Way-finding and signposting: penance or prosthesis, R. Easterby, H. Zwaga (eds), *Information Design*, John Wiley and Sons, New York.

Carter, D., 1976, *Corporate Identity Manuals*, Century Communications Unlimited, Inc. New York.

Carter, S., 1987, *Twentieth Century Type Designers*, Trefoil.

Card, S., Moran, T., Newell, A., 1983, *The Psychology of Human-Computer Interaction*, Lawrence Erlbaum Associates, New Jersey.

C. Brown, M., 1999, *Human-Computer Interface Design Guidelines*, Intellect.

Chizlett, C., Correspondence, 5 February 1999.

Chizlett, C., 1999, Silent Messenger: The Chinese Concept-Script, unpublished.

Cimino, J., 1997, *Intranets; The Surf Within*, Charles River Media, Massachusetts.

Coe, M., 1992, *Breaking the Maya Code*, Thames and Hudson.

Crystal, D., 1971, *Linguistics*, Pelican.

Dair, C., 1967, *Design with Type*, University of Toronto Press, Toronto.

de Bono, E., 1971, *The Mechanism of Mind*, Penguin Books.

de Grandis, L., 1986, *Theory and use of colour*, Blandford Press.

DeFrancis, J,. 1989, *Visible speech – the diverse oneness of writing systems*, University of Hawaii Press, Honolulu.

Design Process for Information Products (Internet). Downloaded from the WWW 6 April 1999. http://www.amanda.com/publications

Dreyfuss, H., 1972, *Symbol Sourcebook*, McGraw-Hill, New York.

Erickson, T., 1990, Interface and the Evolution of Pidgins: Creative Design for the Analytically Inclined. Laural, B. (ed), *The Art of Human-Computer Interface Design*, Addison-Wesley, Massachusetts.

Erickson, T. 1990, Working with Interface Metaphors, B. Laural (ed), *The Art of Human-Computer Interface Design*, Addison-Wesley, Massachusetts.

Foley, J., 1993, *The Guinness Encyclopaedia of Signs and Symbols*, Guinness.

Frutiger, A., 1991, *Signs and Symbols: Their Design and Meaning*, Studio Editions.

Frutiger, A., 1980, *Type Sign Symbol*, ABC Verlag, Zurich.

Gethin, A., Gunnemark, E., 1996, *The Art and Science of Learning Languages*, Intellect.

Goldsmith, E., 1984, *Research into illustration: an approach and a review*, Cambridge University Press.

Gombrich, E., 1975, *The Story of Art*, 12th Edition, Phaidon.

Gorkin, B., Carnase, T., 1995, *The best in digital classic text fonts*, Graphis, New York.

Graphical Symbols Compliant to IEC Standard 417 (Internet). Downloaded from the WWW 16 April 1998 http://w3.hike.te.chiba-u.ac.jp/iec417/ver2.0/html/index.html

Gregory, R., 1970, *The Intelligent Eye*, Weidenfeld & Nicolson.

Hamilton, J., (ed), 1997, *The Totally Scantastic guide to Desktop Scanning*, EPSON.

Hammond, N., 1982, *Ancient Maya Civilisation*, Cambridge University Press.

Harling, P., Edwards, A., 1997, Hand Tension as a Gesture Segmentation Cue, Harling, P., Edwards, A., (eds), *Progress in Gestural Interaction: Proceedings of Gesture Workshop '96*, Springer-Verlag.

Heart Origin (Internet). Downloaded from the WWW 15 October 1998 http://www.symbols.com

Honeywill, P., Thorn, T., Vranch, A., Phillips, M., 1995, The Virtual Studio: Collaboration through digital networks, *Intelligent Tutoring Media* 6 (2), p.63-72.

Houston, S., 1989, *Maya Glyphs*, British Museum Publications.

Hudson, R., 1984, *Invitation to Linguistics*, Martin Robertson.

Hughes, R., (Illustrator), 1997, *MacUser*, 19 September.

Hulbert, A., 1978 *The Grid*, Van Nostrand Reinhold Company, New York.

Ingen-Housz. T., 1996, *The Elephants Memory: Resources Grammer and Syntax*, Kunsthochschule für Medien, Köln.

Jones T., author conversation, University of Texas, Austin, 12 March 1997.

Jones, T., Jones, C., 1995, Maya Hieroglyphic Workbook, Humbolt State University, unpublished.

Kay, A., email conversation, 23 October 1998.

Kay, A., 1990, User Interface: A Personal View, B. Laural (ed), *The Art of Human-Computer Interface Design*, Addison-Wesley, Massachusetts.

Kelly, D., 1976, *Deciphering the Maya Script*, University of Texas Press, Austin.

Kennerly, D., email conversation 30 October 1998.

Kentie, P., 1997, *Web Graphics Tools and Techniques*, Peachpit Press, Berkeley.

Kress, G., 1995, *21st Century A-Z Literacy Handbook*. Preston C., Project Miranda, Institute of Education, London.

Lakoff, G., Johnson, M., 1980, *Metaphors we live by*, University of Chicago Press, Chicago.

Language School (Internet). Downloaded from the WWW 30 August 1998. http://www.syz.com

Linotype, 1989, *Linotype Collection Mergenthaler Type Library*, Linotype AG, Hamburg.

Luna, P., 1992, *Understanding type for desktop publishing*, Blueprint.

Lohse, G., Biolsi, K., Walker, N., Rueter, H., 1994, A Classification of Visual Representations, *Communications of the ACM*, 37 (12), p.36-49, New York.

Love (Internet). Downloaded from the WWW 15 October 1998 http://www.loveatfirstsight.com

Macau International Airport (Internet). Downloaded from the WWW, 20 April 1999. http://www.macau-airport.gov.mo

Making Good Looking WWW GIFs or JPEGs for Multi-Platforms (Internet). Downloaded from the WWW 17 August 1998 http://www.cgsd.com/papers/gamma.web.html

Marcus, A., 1984, Corporate Identity for Iconic Interface Design: The Graphic design Perspective, *Interfaces in Computing*, 2 (b), p.365-378, Elsevier Sequoia, Netherlands.

Marcus, A., 1992, *Graphic Design for Electronic Documents and User Interfaces*, ACM Press.

McDonald's Restaurants (Internet). Downloaded from the WWW 19 November 1998. http://www.mcdonalds.com

McLean, R., (ed), 1995, *Typographers on Type*, Lund Humphries.

McQuail, D., Windahal, S., 1986, *Communication Models: For the study of Mass Communications*, Longman, New York.

Mealing, S., 1991, Talking Pictures, *Intelligent Tutoring Media*, 2 (2) p.63-69.

Mealing, S., Yazdani, M., 1990, A Computer-based Iconic Language, *Intelligent Tutoring Media*, 1 (3), p.133-136.

Metaphor Design and Cultural Diversity in Advanced User Interfaces (Internet). Downloaded from the WWW 6th April 1999. http://www.amanda.com/publication

Miller, L., Johnson, J., 1996, The Xerox Star: An Influential User Interface Design, In M, Rudisill, C. Lewis, P. Polson, T. McKay (eds), *Human-Computer Interface Design: Success Stories, Emerging Methods, and Real-World Context*, California.

Morgan, J., Welton, P., 1986, *See What I Mean*, Edward Arnold.

Neurath, M., 1974, Isotype, *Instructional Science*, 3, Amsterdam.

Neurath, O., 1980, *International picture language/Internationale Bildersprache*, A facsimile reprint of the (1936) English edition, Psyche Miniatures General Series, Kegan Paul, Department of Typography & Graphic Communication, University of Reading.

Olins, W., 1989, *Corporate Identity; Making Business Stratagy Visible Through Design*, Thames and Hudson.

Olson, J., Moran, T., 1996, Mapping the Method Muddle: Guidance in Using Methods for User Interface Design, In M, Rudisill, C. Lewis, P. Polson, T. McKay (eds), *Human-Computer Interface Design: Success Stories, Emerging Methods, and Real-World Context*, California.

Ossner, J., 1990, Transnational Symbols: The Rule of Pictogram Models in the Learning Process, J. Nielson (ed), *Designing User Interfaces for International Use*, Elsevier, Amsterdam.

Ota, Y., 1993, *Pictogram Design: Popular Edition*, Kashiwa Bijutsu Shuppan, Tokyo.

Pettersson, J., 1996, *Grammatogogical Studies: Writing and its Relation to Speech*, Uppsala, Sweden.

Pfizer, Third Party Intranet Development Guidelines, Briefing Document, 19th November 1998, unpublished.

Philip and Alex's Guide to Web Publishing (Internet). Downloaded from the WWW 10 August 1998 http://photo.net

Proline Internet Services (Internet). Downloaded from the WWW 29 October 1998. http://www.proline.co.kr

Pirous, R., Weinman, L., 1997, *Click here*, New Riders Publishing, Indianapolis.

Rabbit in the Moon (Internet). Downloaded from the WWW 19 June 1999 http://www.halfmoon.org

Rheingold, H., 1990, An Interview with Don Norman, B. Laural (ed), *The Art of Human-Computer Interface Design*, Addison-Wesley, Massachusetts.

Reuters (Internet). Downloaded from the WWW, 26 November 1998. http://www.reuters.com

Salomon, G., 1990, New Uses for Color, B. Laural (ed), *The Art of Human-Computer Interface Design*, Addison-Wesley, Massachusetts.

Sampson, G., 1985, Writing Systems, Hutchinson.

Sano, D., 1996, *Designing large-scale websites: a visual design methodology*, John Wiley & Sons, New York.

Sassoon, R., 1993, *Computers and Typography*, Intellect.

Sassoon, R., Gaur, A., 1997, *Signs, symbols and icons; Pre-history to the computer age*, Intellect.

Schele, L., Miller, M., 1986, *The Blood of Kings*, George Braziller Inc., Fort Worth.

Schuler, D., 1996, *New Community Networks; Wired for change*, Addison-Wesley, Massachusetts.

Scrivener, S., Vernon, S., 1995, Design Net: Translational design project work at a distance, *Digital Creativity*, Proceedings of the 1st Conference on Computers in Art & Design Education, University of Brighton.

Shneiderman, B., email conversation, 23 October 1988.

Shneiderman, B., 1995, *Sparks of Innovation in Human-Computer Interaction*, Ablex Publishing Corporation, New Jersey.

Signals, *A-Z of Typography*, Channel 4.

Singapore Changi International Airport (Internet). Downloaded from the WWW 20 April 1999. http://www.changi.airport.com.sg

Straight from the Heart (Internet). Downloaded from the WWW 15th October 1998 http://www.rice.edu/armadillo/sciacademy/medhigh/heart.htm

Stuart, D., 1984, A note on the 'hand-scattering glyph, J. Justen, L. Campbell (eds), *Phoneticism in Mayan Hieroglyphic Writing, Institute for Mesoamerican Studies*, State University of New York, Albany.

Stubbs, M., 1980, *Language and Literacy: The Sociolinguistics of Reading and Writing*, Routledge & Kegan Paul.

Sub-Pixel Font Rendering Technology (Internet). Downloaded from the WWW 11 March 1999. http://www.grc.com/ctwhat.htm

Symbols.com (Internet). Downloaded from the WWW 3 December 1998 http://www.symbols.com

Take Welness to Heart (Internet). Downloaded from the WWW 15 October 1998 http://women.americanheart.org

Thompson, E., 1972, *Maya Hieroglyphs without Tears*, Trustees of the British Museum.

Tognazzini, B., 1990, Consistency, B. Laural (ed), *The Art of Human-Computer Interface Design.*, Addison-Wesley, Massachusetts.

Tourist Guide to Vancouver (Internet). Downloaded from the WWW 30 August 1998. http://www.discouvervancouver.com

Wang, W., 1981, Language structure and optimal orthography, Tenz, O., Singer, H. (eds), *Perception of Print*, Lawrence Erlbaum Associates, Hillside, New Jersey.

Werkman, C., 1974, *Trademarks: Their creation, psychology and perception*, Longman.

Wetherell, A., 1978, Some factors affecting spatial memory for route information, R. Easterby, H. Zwaga (eds), *Information Design*, John Wiley and Sons, New York.

Why Do Images Appear Darker on Some Displays? (Internet). Downloaded from the www 15 August 1998. http://www.vtiscan.com/~rwb/gamma.html

Williams, M., 1994, *MacUser*, 10 (15)

Wilson, H., 1993, *Understanding Hieroglyphs*, Michael O'Mara.

Wilson, P., 1991, *Computer Supported Cooperative Work*, Intellect.

Yazdani, M., Goring, D., 1990, *Iconic Communication*, Department of Computer Science, Exeter University.

Young Choi, J., email conversation, 26 November 1998

Zwaga, H., Easterby, R., 1978, Developing effective symbols for public information, R. Easterby, H. Zwaga (eds), *Information Design*, John Wiley and Sons.

Index

Abstract 24, 105, 106
Actor 119, 121
Affix 24
Aicher's grid 102
American National Standards
       Institute 159
Andorra 173
Angola 166
Anti-aliasing 66
Apple Lisa 14, 55
ARC 125-128, 134, 154
Aries 86
Arrows 49, 54, 115, 116, 119
Associative field 119
Asymmetrical 71, 72
Australia 171
Austria 173
Aztec 121, 122

Back margin 70
Ball Player 29
Baseline 99
Basic English 48
Beck, H. 150
Blissymbolics 117, 118, 122, 134
Body alphabet 51, 103, 111
Border 69-71
Brazil 180
Broken Black letter 181
Bulgaria 173
Burlington Northern 89
Buxton, B. 87

Calender Round 18, 19
Canada 145, 172, 175
Capital letters 93
Cham Balhum II 29, 30
China 15, 168
Chizlett, C. 15, 62
Coe, M. 15, 25, 27
Cognitive Walkthrough 125
Colour 64, 90, 94, 97, 150, 151
Comprehension 151
Conflict 64, 65, 68
Consistency 143
Consonent-vowel 34
Consumption of signs 155
Content 153
Contrast 64, 65, 82, 83, 85, 95
Corporate identity 85, 88, 116, 158
Costa Rica 176
CRT 67, 155
Curves 100
Cyprus 174

de Bono, E. 161-162
Declarative sentences 20
DeFrancis, J. 31, 45-46
destination indicator 119
Digital fonts 76
Discrimination Principle 144
Disorientation 153
Distance Marker 19
document icons 55
Dreyfuss, H. 63, 64, 115, 117
Dynamic icon behaviour 126

Edge definition 69
Egypt 166, 172
Egyptian hieroglyph 91
Egyptian hieroglyphics 15
Elephants Memory 118-122
Email 110, 122
Emoticon 123
England 175
Eras 93, 94, 95
Erickson, T. 13, 51, 91
eWorld 135, 145, 152-156

Facial expression 123
Fiji 171
Florida 178
France 126, 174
Frutiger, A. 36, 53, 62, 95, 96,
    100, 101, 102, 120

Gamma 67
Gerbner's general model 141
Germany 174
Gestalt 61, 62
Gestures 58
Goldsmith, E. 44, 45, 151, 156
Gregory, R. 15
Grid architecture 89
Guatemala 176
Hamilton, J. 13
Harmony 64, 65, 82
Hewlett-Packard 40, 60
Hinting 78
Home screen 127, 130
Hue 64, 83, 90, 94

Ideographic 18, 121
Ideographs 122
Idiomatic 118
IEC 39
Image perception 156
Indexical 160
India 168
Indonesia 169

Infix 80
Interchangeable elements 103,
    111
Internet 105, 106, 124, 162, 180,
    182
Intranet 104, 105
ISO 39, 42, 52, 53, 54, 58, 115,
    158, 159, 160, 161, 182
Isotype 44, 47, 48, 52, 102, 144
Internet Service Providers 162
Israel 168

Jaguar 35
Jamaica 176
Japanese signs 15
Java script 126
Jerma Palace Hotel 150
Johnston, E. 75

Kan Hok Chitam II 29
Kay, A. 46, 61, 102, 112
Kelly, D. 56
Kenya 166, 172
Kern edit 79
Knorosov, Y. 16
Kobayashi, K. 87
Kress, G. 14

Laurel, B. 46
Lebanon 168
Legibility 75
Letterform 106
Lexicon 40, 52, 53, 58, 83, 112,
    113, 117, 118, 122, 128
Line segments 100
Literacy 97
Lloyds TSB 158, 160, 161
Logo 69, 116, 117, 146
Logogram 27, 34
Long Count 18, 19
Lowercase 73

Macau International Airport 30
MacUser 135, 146, 147, 148,
        149, 150, 156
Magazine 70, 83, 105, 146
Magazine designers 146
Main Sign 23
Malaysia 169
Marcus, A. 55, 90, 125, 141,
        151, 155
Mathematical centre 72
Maya hieroglyphs 16, 18, 22, 27,
        28, 30, 56, 58, 64, 81, 86
Maya syntax 117
McDonalds 78, 107
Meaningfulness 41
Mesoamerican 99, 100, 121
Metamerism 90
Metaphor 23, 44, 83, 118, 141
Mexico 177
Microsoft 60, 66, 136, 139, 140
Mixtec 121, 122
Monolines 93
Mood 95, 99, 100
Morison, S. 75, 76
Morphological 34
Mouse-up 126
Munich Olympic symbols 102

n-mail 106
Namibia 167
Natural written language 45, 52
Navigation points 126, 129
Navigational signing systems 50
Navigational technique 146
Netscape Communication
        Corporation 153
Neurath 47, 48, 50, 52, 80, 102,
        144, 156
New Hampshire 178
New York 178
New Zealand 171, 180
Nexon 105, 106
Nicaragua 177

North American Indian 115, 118
Northern Ireland 175

Object 21, 23, 24, 80, 156
Olins, W. 88, 89, 116
Oops button 127
Optical centre 71, 73
Optical character balance 92
Optically correct 100
Oregon 179
Ota, Y. 54, 144

Pakistan 169, 172
Partial writing 45
Paths 100
Patial memory 142
Penis-title 33
Pfizer 104, 105
Philippines 170
Phoenician 31
Phonetic 25, 27, 34, 57, 81,
        123
Phonetic table 31, 32
Phonograms 34
Pictograms 121
Pictographic 120
Pictorial 117
Piedras Negras 30
Place 153
Plural infliction 119
Post Office 162
Postfix 23, 80
Pragmatic 94, 154
Pre-cuniform Sumerian 31, 120
Prefix 23, 80
Proline 105
Proskouriakoff, T. 16
Proximity 61
Psychology 125
Public Information 160

QuarkXPress 42, 78, 143
Questionnaire 39, 41, 43, 57

Recovery time 130
Reordering the locations 152
Representational 34, 106, 127,
    129, 133-134, 141
Restriction 115
Retroactive inhibition 142
Reuters 110
RGB 151
Rode Island 179
Roman letterform 99, 100
Russia 170

Sampson 15
Sans serif 77, 93, 95
Saturation 83, 90
Scattering blood 26
Schele, L. 16
Schramm model 82
Self-explaining 123
Semantic 100, 154, 155, 159
Semantic interference 144
Semantography 117
Serifs 71
Shinbiro 107, 109
Side-bearing 79
Simple words 45, 48, 50, 51
SmallTalk 46, 102
Smily face 110
South Africa 167
South Carolina 179
Spatial harmony 85
Spatial memory 94, 130, 141
Static 129
Sub-pixel 66
Sun Microsystems 46
Superfix 23
Switzerland 174
Symbol 39, 45, 50, 52, 57, 85,
    86, 88, 91, 94, 95, 96, 99,
    102, 103, 111, 116, 117,
    158
Symmetrical 71
Syntax 37, 61, 64, 93, 102, 111

Thailand 170
Tokyo Olympic games 102, 144
Tonga 110
Track and monitor learning 127
Traffic signs 115
Triangles 116
Type 36, 74, 77, 76, 92, 99, 122

Uneven width monolines 93
Utilitarian language 122

Valentine cards 86
Verb 19, 20, 21, 56, 141, 142
Visual grammar 118
Visual oscillation 70
Visual Reading Order 61
Visual sentence 118

W3C (World Wide Web
Consortium) 104, 182
Wang, W. 15
Wars of the Roses 144
Water 91, 92, 94
Web interfaces 126, 156
Wisconsin 179
Word 136, 140

x height 73, 76, 92
Xerox 159
Xerox 8010 'Star' Information
System 46
Xerox PARC 61, 102
Xerox Star 55
Xunantunich 96, 97

Yaxchilán 17

Zimbabwe 167
Zwaga, H., and Easterby, R. 52,
53, 115, 158